Cre8ive
ICT

Other titles of interest

Learning on the Net
A Practical Guide to Enhancing Learning in Primary Classrooms
Alan Pritchard
1-84312-082-8

Understanding and Teaching the ICT National Curriculum
Franc Potter and Carol Darbyshire
1-84312-133-66

Creativity in the Primary Curriculum
Russell Jones and Dominic Wyse
1-85346-871-1

Unlocking Creativity
A Teacher's Guide to Creativity Across the Curriculum
Robert Fisher
1-84312-092-5

Cre8ive ICT

Antony Smith and Simon Willcocks

 David Fulton Publishers

David Fulton Publishers Ltd
The Chiswick Centre, 414 Chiswick High Road, London W4 5TF

www.fultonpublishers.co.uk

First published in Great Britain in 2004 by David Fulton Publishers
10 9 8 7 6 5 4 3 2 1

David Fulton Publishers is a division of Granada Learning Limited, part of ITV plc.

British Library Cataloguing in Publication Data
A catalogue record for this book is available from the British Library.

ISBN 1 84312 136 0

Typeset by FiSH Books, London
Printed and bound in Spain

Contents

Acknowledgements

We would like to thank our senior colleagues at Halsford Park Primary School, St Mary's Catholic Primary School and Fonthill Lodge Preparatory School for the opportunities they provided for us to develop our interest in ICT. We would also like to thank the pupils who engaged so enthusiastically with these activities, in particular those who made their work available for inclusion in this book. Sincere thanks to Helen Fairlie for believing in our vision for the book and working with us to bring it to fruition. Many thanks also to Lis Mason for all her invaluable comments and feedback on each draft of the manuscript. Finally, we would like to thank our families, who have remained interested and supportive through all the book's metamorphoses.

Introduction

Learning objectives

The activities in this book provide creative and imaginative departure points for children to develop and apply core ICT skills to their wider studies and interests. They are not intended to be worked through sequentially, although some tasks do pursue complementary themes and can be used together. Rather, each unit is intended to provide a stand alone activity that can be incorporated into wider classroom- or home-based learning. Together, the activities provide for extension work in Key Stage 2 ICT, while also providing cross-curricular links to literacy, numeracy and the humanities. It is hoped that they have been written in a straightforward way so that pupils and their parents and teachers can engage with the tasks easily and efficiently.

Pupils are given opportunities to:

- undertake research about a range of concepts across the curriculum via a variety of sources including internet sources;
- develop understanding of mathematical concepts/manipulation of geometrical shapes in space;
- develop extended writing and editing skills;
- develop an appreciation of the works of a variety of artists and how they influenced future generations of artists;
- develop an understanding of how core ICT skills can be applied imaginatively across mathematics, English, history, science and art;
- work on their own at the computer on an extended classroom or personal project;
- develop their own 2-D and 3-D computer generated art;
- develop an understanding of how art can be reinterpreted via a modern medium.

How to use this book

This book has been designed to be used in a number of ways. One important aim is to provide ideas for teachers who wish to fully integrate ICT into a creative and varied curriculum rather than teach it as a discrete subject. However, the book can equally be used by parents who wish to support their child's learning at home, through providing fun and challenging activities that children will be motivated to pursue outside a formal learning environment. The activities are all based around word processing, art and spreadsheet software (Microsoft) which are commonly available to PC users both at home and in the classroom. Each can be incorporated into whole class teaching across a number of topics, or can be utilised in smaller group work or individual learning.

The first section of each activity is designed with the child learner in mind, and provide all the instructions needed to work through the task. Screen shots are provided to help the child navigate around the various computer programs. Many activities include examples of other children's work, and extension activities presented as 'challenges'. These pages can be photocopied and provided to each child working on the activity.

Each activity then concludes with a parent/teacher section which provides additional information and, for teachers, suggestions about how the activities may be used in the classroom.

The authors

Antony Smith and Simon Willcocks are both teachers working in primary schools. Antony is currently responsible for developing ICT at St Mary's Primary School in Worthing, having previously developed this curriculum area at Halsford Park Primary School in East Grinstead. Simon has held a number of posts of curriculum development. He has been head of an international school that had Technology College Trust status, developed an enrichment curriculum via ICT at Halsford Park and now has a similar role at Fonthill Lodge Preparatory School in East Grinstead. Both Antony and Simon have backgrounds in art and design.

CHAPTER 1

Core Areas: More to maths than meets the pi...

There is more to maths than just crunching numbers, although that can be fun (honest!). In these units we have primarily developed work on space and shape: the ideas are familiar to a lot of us but we have placed them in an ICT context. We have identified significant artists to provide additional cross-curricular links. There are also opportunities for a bit of number crunching and even some work using formulae. The activities can be extended into some sophisticated work on the properties of shape and can result in some stunning artwork.

It's only words?
The literacy activities predominantly use creative writing as either a starting point or as the focus for a finished piece of work. They also bring in aspects of mathematics as another means of looking at writing. All the activities make creative use of Word and help to develop a deeper understanding of writing, as well as exploring how the grammar and spelling tools in Word can be utilised to produce original work.

Cool Curves and Rockin' Riley

You will need: Microsoft Word and access to pictures and information about the artists Yvarel Vasarely and Bridget Riley.

This is a great task that helps you get to know more about the properties of shape, whilst creating optical illusions to dazzle your friends with. It uses the Curves of Pursuit idea: each square, as it rotates, gets progressively smaller.

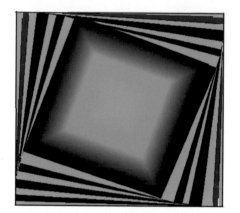

Laura, Year 6

Amy, Year 6

The Task

Take a look at paintings by **Yvarel Vasarely**. He was an 'op artist'. That means he made pictures to create an optical illusion. You can see how he uses the Curves of Pursuit idea to create a piece of work called 'untitled'.

You can create some great 'Vasarely' style art. By the way, another artist, Victor de Vasarely, is worth looking at too but don't get them confused.

Left-click on the 'Rectangle' in the 'AutoShapes' toolbar facility. Left-click the cursor on the screen and drag it to try to create a perfect square. The outside edge of a square is known as the perimeter. Make it large enough to fill the screen.

Rectangle Facility

When you have drawn your square, mark four points, using 'Line' along the perimeter of the square as shown in the diagram. Then join them. Repeat the same process and see what happens. 'Line' is also on the 'AutoShapes' toolbar.

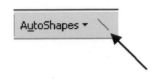

Line Facility

You can also do this investigation with equilateral triangles – can you work out how it's done?

Where do you think you might find triangle shapes?

Have another look at the examples by Amy and Laura above. See how they have filled in the last square? Can you work out how they have done that?

Now that you have tried all these techniques can you combine all three to make your own computer generated Op Art? Here are two examples that we have made using **Bridget Riley** as our inspiration. She liked to use simple shapes and lines to create optical illusions. We reckon you could create some great ideas using your imagination and 'AutoShapes'. If you get hooked on the idea of Curves of Pursuit here is a great website run by a guy called Ivars Petersen (*www.maa.org*).

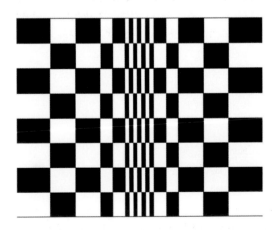

Squares

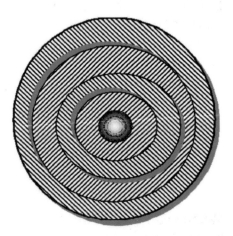

Circles

Have a look at Daniel's art below. Brilliant, isn't it?

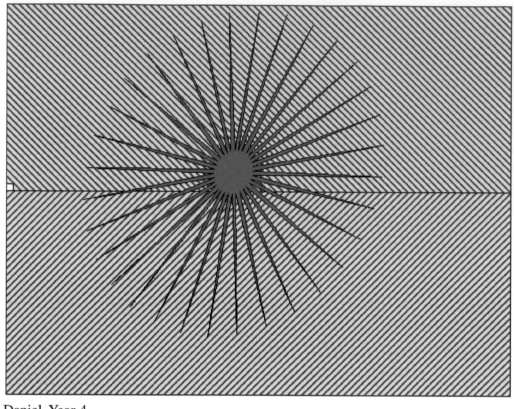

Daniel, Year 4

Here's a challenge: we used 'Paint' to fill in the blocks in our example. Can you work out how we did it? Some of the other art tasks will help you.

✏ Notes for Parents and Teachers

This is a fun activity that encourages precision and attention to detail. It exposes the pupils to an unusual tradition in art and the work of some great artists. Children enjoy optical illusions, and this task gives them the opportunity to experiment, have fun and learn some mathematical concepts on the way.

This task can be done either individually or as a group task in the ICT suite. It is great for giving pupils the skills to create shapes accurately and precisely, and provides a fun dimension to any maths project on the properties of shape. It also introduces pupils to the concept of transformation of shapes and images and supports work on quadrants and grids. Equally, it works really well to introduce and extend the language related to shapes.

We have also used it successfully as an extension activity on units of work where children have been investigating how the eye and the brain work in relation to optical illusions.

To repeat the Curves of Pursuit task with triangles, the process is basically the same. Create an equilateral triangle from AutoShapes and make points at equal differences from the vertices like so:

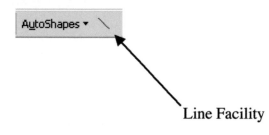

Line Facility

National Curriculum Links for Key Stage 2

Numeracy
Ma3) Shape, space and measures: 2c, 3b and 3c
Art
2b and 5c

TOPIC LINKS

Optical Illusions
The Eye and How it Works
Modern Art
Shapes and Space
Bridget Riley
Vasarely

Marvellous Mystic Rose

You will need: Microsoft Word and/or Paint

The Task

Look at the illustrations below. Aren't they brilliant? They look quite complicated but they are really easy to create. A mystic rose is a mathematical design where equally spaced points on the circumferance are joined to each other.

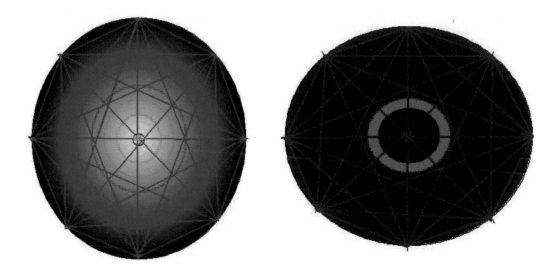

Create a large circle from the 'Oval' facility in 'AutoShapes'. The outside edge of the circle is called the circumference.

Oval Facility

Starting at the top (the 12 o'clock position), mark points at equal distances apart around the circumference using the 'Line' facility:

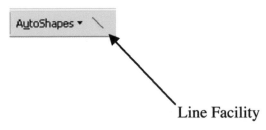

Line Facility

You can mark as many points as you like but to begin with you can follow the example above or mark your points according to the numbers on a clock.

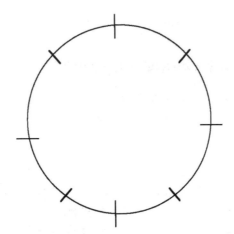

Now join your points. Using 'Line' connect the top point to the one on its immediate left.

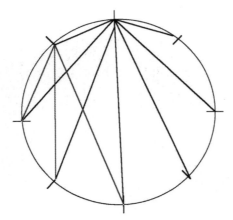

Then, still working from the top point, connect the top point to every other point on the circumference.

When you have done that connect the next point to the right of the top point to all the other points. Carry on connecting all points to all points. You will notice that you are connecting one less point each time – can you think why this is?

If you use the 'Line Colour' facility to change the lines radiating from each point the job will be easier and make a really snazzy design. Draw the line and then click on 'Line Colour' and choose the colour you want.

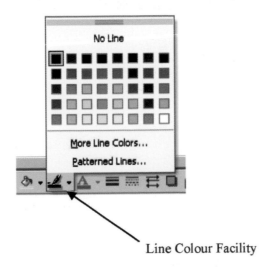

Line Colour Facility

If you do the job in 'Paint' then you can fill in the internal shapes using the 'Fill Colour' facility.

The more points you use on the circumference, the more intricate your design. You can always tell if you have created the perfect mystic rose: if all the lines that are opposite each other on the circumference cross precisely in the middle it is perfect.

Challenge

Your challenge is to increase the number of points on the circumference and make all your roses perfect. Matthew's example below is almost perfect. Have another look at the examples on p. 6. These have used some features in Word to develop their work. Can you work out how they have been done?

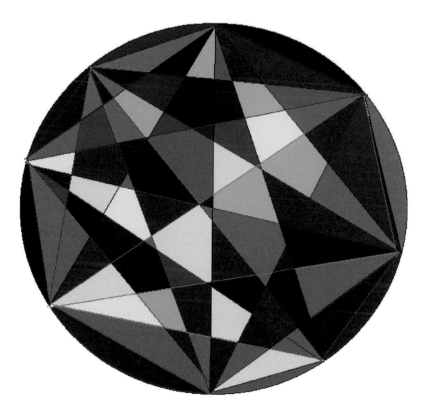

Matthew, Year 4

Notes for Parents and Teachers

This activity encourages creativity, precision and attention to detail. It also engages children with a number of the geometric concepts required by the KS2 numeracy scheme of work. There are also a number of artistic traditions based on maths, for example Islamic art, and this activity provides a useful introduction to this area of study.

In class, the task can be done as extension/support work done on space and shape. It also provides a departure point for a number of investigations into pattern and the relationship between the frequency of lines being connected to points on the circumference. It can also be used with more able children to look into the properties of circles, including pi.

National Curricum Links for Key Stage 2

Numeracy
Ma2) 1i, Ma3
Art
2b and 5c

TOPIC LINKS

Properties of Circles
Geometry
Space and Shape
Islamic Art
Compass Points
Colour Matching

Crazy Curved Stitching

You will need: Microsoft Word and/or Paint

'Space and Shape' is a major attainment target in the National Curriculum for maths. These ideas will allow you to have loads of fun creating all sorts of designs whilst covering important aspects of Space and Shape.

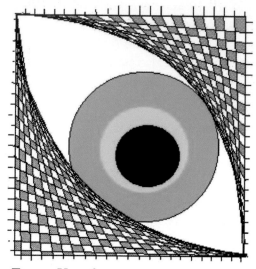

Tanera, Year 6

The Task

Use the 'Line' facility to draw a vertical (top to bottom) axis on the left-hand side of your screen. Then use the same facility to draw a horizontal (left to right) axis. Depending on how big you want to work you may need to keep checking your progress on 'Print Preview'.

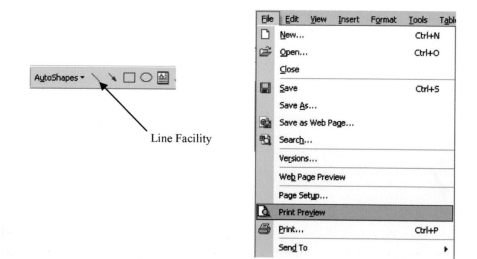

Line Facility

Remember that the horizontal axis is referred to as the 'x' axis and the vertical axis is referred to as the 'y' axis. Try to make sure that the axes are the same length.

Still using 'Line', mark small 'points' along each axis. If you mark 10 points along the 'x' axis you must mark 10 points along the 'y' axis.

Now join the points. You do it like this: join the top 'point' on the 'y' axis to the point furthest left on the 'x' axis. Then join the next to top point on the 'y' axis to the next furthest left on the 'x' axis.

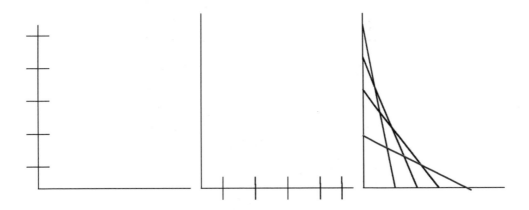

Once you have finished you will have created a 'curved' effect using only straight lines.

Once you have the hang of the technique you can make some really sophisticated designs. You can use the 'Line Colour' facility to change the colours in your design.

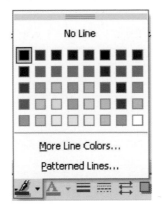

Challenge

If you go through the same process in 'Paint' you can fill in the internal shapes to make some brilliant designs. Try experimenting with complementary colours, blue and purple perhaps, or opposite colours like blue and yellow.

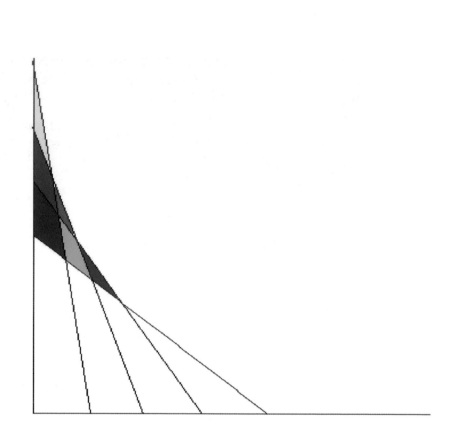

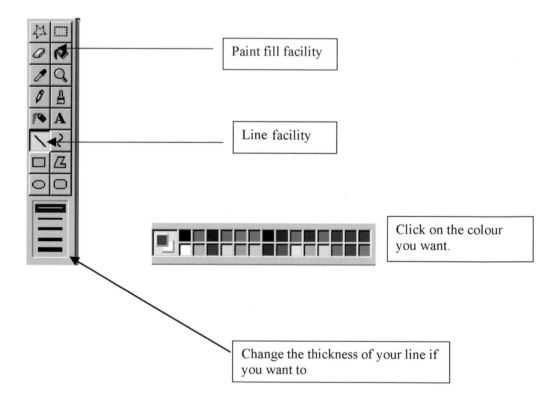

Paint fill facility

Line facility

Click on the colour
you want.

Change the thickness of your line if
you want to

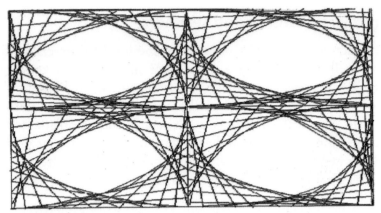

Matthew, Year 4

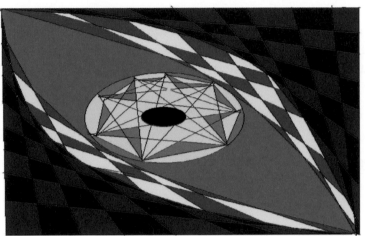

Taylor, Year 4

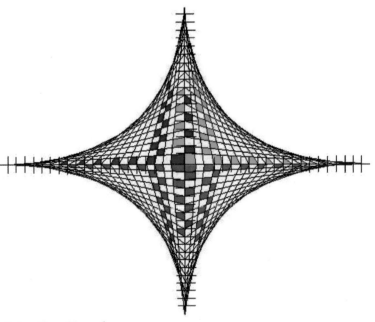

Sebastian, Year 6

If this idea has you sewn up, then visit *www.montessoriworld.org*. There are some great ideas for you to look at.

✎ Notes for Parents and Teachers

This is a fun activity that really encourages the need for precision and attention to detail as well as embracing a number of mathematical concepts. Children really enjoy the process and express real amazement as the curved appearance materialises before their eyes. Once the children are familiar with the process they are able to create their own elaborate and sophisticated designs by increasing the number of axes and arranging them in different positions and by increasing the number of points along each axis. Some of the more able pupils have experimented with combining this activity with the mystic rose task.

This task can be used in the classroom as an individual activity or as a group exercise in the ICT suite. It introduces pupils to aspects of the language of space, shape, plotting and graph construction and coordinates. The task can be extended into work on quadrants and if you number the points in each axis on a design like Sebastian's then the children can start getting into negative numbers as well. The more able pupils will be able to come up with some incredibly precise and sophisticated designs and the activity really does stimulate the imagination.

National Curriculum Links for Key Stage 2

Maths
Ma3) Shape, space and measures: 2c, 3b and 3c
Art
2b and 5c

TOPIC LINKS

Geometry
Quadrants
Coordinates
Negative Numbers
Space and Shape
Quadrilaterals
Optical Illusions

Terrible Text Challenge

You will need: Microsoft Word or any other word processing program.

This is an unusual way of using a computer's spellchecker to learn about homophones and why some words, although sounding correct, are in fact wrong.

Homophone: a word that sounds the same as another word but which is spelled differently and has a different meaning (e.g. pair, pear).

The Task

Read this closely:

KNOW MORE MISS STEAKS
I have a spelling checker,
it came with my PC
It plainly marks for my revue
Mistakes I cannot sea.
I have run this poem threw it
I'm sure your please to no.
It's letter perfect in its weigh
My checker tolled me sew
(Stephen Hume, *The Vancouver Sun*, 21/06/99)

It all makes sense and it beats the computer's spell check, yet it is clearly not correct. Can you write your own short story or poem using homophones that will beat the computer's spell check?

Need help carrying out a spell check? Then follow the instructions below. There are three ways to check your spelling:

1. Select 'Spelling and Grammar' by left clicking on 'Tools'.

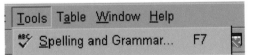

2. Press F7 on the keyboard.

3. Click on the 'ABC' section of the toolbar.

List of useful homophones

buoy	boy	hour	our
moor	more	wait	weight
weigh	way	sea	see
their	there	fare	fair
role	roll	bough	bow

Extension activity

Can you find any other homophones or other words that can be split or combined like mistake – miss steak?

Here is an example of one girl's work.

Bus Stop

I weight for an hour under the cold bus stop, and then I meet a buoy showing me a roll of his acting. In the distance we both see a storm of heir pass our way. They're we standing in the middle of nowhere and the buses have stopped, the only thing I can do is hold my hare bow tightly in my hand. Then I see a wave of the ocean see, like a flood has started.

Georgina, Year 6

✍ Notes for Parents and Teachers

This activity encourages children of all abilities to actually read what they have written, by recognising some of the common mistakes that they often make. It also helps children to understand that while ICT can be useful when correcting work, it has limitations and humans ultimately need to know how to spell! The creative potential to play with words appeals to children's natural curiosity and this task can be a real mental workout for linguistically inclined learners.

This activity can be used as a stand-alone resource for individual children or can be incorporated into whole class teaching. In the later case, the activity can be incorporated into the literacy hour as part of the word level work, or can be part of a series of lessons on creative and nonsense writing.

National Curriculum Links for Key Stage 2

This activity covers:
ICT
1b and 1c
English
(Writing comprehension)
1b, 1d and 2d

TOPIC LINKS

Nonsense Writing
Homophones
Poetry
Spike Milligan
Lewis Carroll

Cracking Codes

You will need: Microsoft Word

Code: a system of words, letters, figures, or symbols, used to represent others for secrecy

The Task

Word has a nice little feature that allows you to insert strange and unusual symbols into a piece of writing. You can use this to create your own TOP SECRET code to share with your friends.

This is how you do it:

Go to 'Insert' then 'Symbol' and play around with inserting symbols into your text.

Here's one example:

> Go to ☞ 'Insert' then ☞ 'Symbol' and play around with inserting symbols into your text. I've used a hand in my sentence.

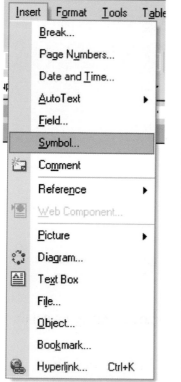

Now create a table with 2 columns and 27 rows.

Go to the top of the page and select Table, then Insert then Table.

Now choose the number of rows and columns.

Put each letter of the alphabet on the left-hand column and assign a symbol to represent it on the right.

Here is an example of just the first three letters of the alphabet.

a	✂
b	✠
c	♉

Once you have completed all the letters and symbols, save it and print it off. Now you can make up a secret message and send it to a friend.

You could e-mail it to your friend and attempt to crack each other's codes or exchange your codes.

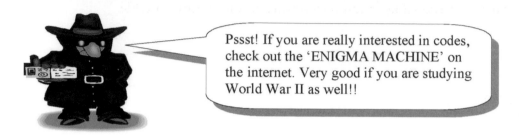

Pssst! If you are really interested in codes, check out the 'ENIGMA MACHINE' on the internet. Very good if you are studying World War II as well!!

If you are really interested in tracking these ideas down a little bit more then visit *www.mckoss.org* to download your own enigma machine. If you want to see what the Enigma machine looked like and learn more about it then visit *www.math.arizona.edu.*

Here's another idea to try. If you get bored with inserting symbols separately, why not assign a key on the keypad to a symbol? Go to 'Insert' then 'Symbol'. You will need to click on the short cut key then choose the Ctrl key plus a letter from the alphabet and you are away.

Cracking Codes Example

©	Ð=ëЖ	Ω=εЖ	¢%¶Δ=¢Δ	*©ΔÐ	ΔÐЖ
I	have	made	contact	with	the

=¥©Ж¶!	ΔÐЖ©+		Ω©!!©%¶	©!	
aliens	their		mission	is	...

✎ Notes for Parents and Teachers

This hidden facility on the 'Word' toolbar and 'Table' facility can be combined in an interesting way to allow children to understand codes and languages.

The activity could be used when teaching the topic on World War II or as a means of introducing children to setting and formatting a table.

National Curriculum Links for Key Stage 2

Literacy
En3) Writing
10
History
11b
ICT
1c

TOPIC LINKS

World War II
Spies and Espionage
The Enigma Machine
Hieroglyphics
Runes

Proof of the Pudding

You will need: Microsoft Word

There are some interesting facts you can find out about different stories. Microsoft Word can tell you how 'readable' a story is. This means how easy it is to read.

Readability statistics

This is a scale based on the number of words per sentence and sentences per paragraph. It rates text on a 100-point scale. The higher the score, the easier it is to understand the document. For most standard documents, you should aim for a score of approximately 60 to 70.

The Task

Take a piece of writing and go to 'Tools'. Once you have the 'Spelling and Grammar' window up, go to options and click on 'Show readability statistics'.

You can find out how 'readable' a book is as a percentage.

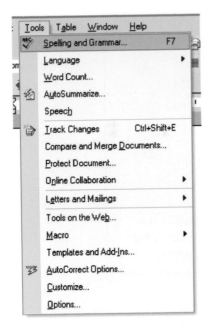

The Cyclone

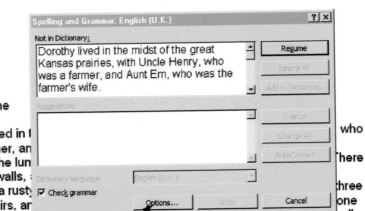

Dorothy lived in t‍‍‍‍‍‍‍‍‍‍‍‍‍‍‍‍‍‍‍‍‍‍‍‍ who
was a farmer, an‍‍‍‍‍‍‍‍‍‍
small, for the lum‍‍‍‍‍‍‍‍‍‍‍ here
were four walls, ‍‍‍‍‍‍‍‍‍‍‍
contained a rusty‍‍‍‍‍‍‍‍‍‍‍ three
or four chairs, an‍‍‍‍‍‍‍‍‍‍‍ one
corner, and Dorothy a little bed in another corner. There was no garret at all,
and no cellar--except a small hole dug in the ground, called a cyclone cellar,
where the family could go in case one of those great whirlwinds arose, mighty
enough to crush any building in its path. It was reached by a trap door in the
middle of the floor, from which a ladder led down into the small, dark hole.
by L. Frank Baum

```
┌─────────────────────────────────────────────────┐
│ Readability Statistics                   ? │ X │ │
├─────────────────────────────────────────────────┤
│  Counts                                         │
│    Words                              170       │
│    Characters                         706       │
│    Paragraphs                           3       │
│    Sentences                            6       │
│                                                 │
│  Averages                                       │
│    Sentences per Paragraph            6.0       │
│    Words per Sentence                27.3       │
│    Characters per Word                4.0       │
│                                                 │
│  Readability                                    │
│    Passive Sentences                  33%       │
│    Flesch Reading Ease               72.1       │
│    Flesch-Kincaid Grade Level         9.0       │
│                                                 │
│                              ┌──────────┐       │
│                              │    OK    │       │
│                              └──────────┘       │
└─────────────────────────────────────────────────┘
```

You can now choose a favourite classic story, copy and cut and paste the first page into Word and do a readability check on it. You can then compare a range of your favourite authors to see who is the most readable. You can also prove it!

If you are feeling really clever, you could write your own story and see how readable you can make it.

Take a look on the internet and put into your search engine 'free online children's stories'.

Then look at 'The Children's Literature Web Guide'.

Then go to 'Classics for young people'.

Check out the example below:
Here's one that we did. We wanted to know how readable the 'The Wizard of Oz' is.

The Cyclone

Dorothy lived in the midst of the great Kansas prairies, with Uncle Henry, who was a farmer, and Aunt Em, who was the farmer's wife. Their house was small, for the lumber to build it had to be carried by wagon many miles. There were four walls, a floor and a roof, which made one room; and this room contained a rusty looking cookstove, a cupboard for the dishes, a table, three or four chairs, and the beds. Uncle Henry and Aunt Em had a big bed in one corner, and Dorothy a little bed in another corner. There was no garret at all, and no cellar – except a small hole dug in the ground, called a cyclone cellar, where the family could go in case one of those great whirlwinds arose, mighty enough to crush any building in its path. It was reached by a trap door in the middle of the floor, from which a ladder led down into the small, dark hole.

by L. Frank Baum

The answer is 72.1 (not very!)

```
┌─────────────────────────────────────────────────────┐
│ Readability Statistics                      [?][X]    │
├─────────────────────────────────────────────────────┤
│ ┌ Counts ─────────────────────────────────────────┐ │
│     Words                               164          │
│     Characters                          682          │
│     Paragraphs                            1          │
│     Sentences                             6          │
│                                                       │
│ ┌ Averages ───────────────────────────────────────┐ │
│     Sentences per Paragraph             6.0          │
│     Words per Sentence                  27.3         │
│     Characters per Word                 4.0          │
│                                                       │
│ ┌ Readability ────────────────────────────────────┐ │
│     Passive Sentences                   16%          │
│     Flesch Reading Ease                 72.1         │
│     Flesch-Kincaid Grade Level          9.0          │
│                                                       │
│                                    ┌──────────┐      │
│                                    │    OK    │      │
│                                    └──────────┘      │
└─────────────────────────────────────────────────────┘
```

Reliability statistics for 'The Wizard of Oz'

Here are a few examples by other children who have tried to expand their sentences and have used the readability statistics to check the number of words per sentence.

Adventure at Sea

As I started to fish my boat started to shake. All of a sudden my boat was filling up with water. Shatter! My boat smashed into loads of pieces. I kept on swimming, then I stopped and had a look around, nothing there. Suddenly up came a bloodthirsty shark. Arrrh! I swam as fast as I could. Then in front of me was an island I picked up the shark and throw it into the sea. The shark swam off. What was I going to do stranded on this heat wave island?

Words per sentence   8.2
Characters per word   3.7

Deep in the Jungle

I can hardly wait for the warm, bright sun of Hawaii to shine on my face. It will be paradise, at least I have all that to look forward to, I mean if I ever get to the check in desk. I've been waiting for in this queue for four hours; I won't get time to do any duty free shopping! But the check in is right next to Costa Coffee, yuk, I hate the smell of coffee. Finally the check in is free.

Lewis, Year 6

Words per sentence   16.8
Characters per word   3.5

Can you work out the readability of this sentence?

'The circumspective panoramic dimensions of the Kilimanjaro geological manifestations known as mountains are undeniably dazzling beyond the spandex busting superlatives judiciously employed by over zealous journalists.'

✍ Notes for Parents and Teachers

Using a computer to give a statistical analysis of writing is an unusual activity but one which many children find fascinating. I gave my class dictionaries and challenged them to come up with paragraphs that had the highest number of characters per word.

Alternatively I've used the passive sentence statistics when teaching about active and passive sentences. It is a great way for the children to instantly see if they can turn a paragraph of active sentences into passive sentences. Children will need to know how to cut and paste for this activity.

Finally, I have recently given my class a story which I have asked them to re-write, using fewer than a hundred words. Using a spellchecker certainly beats counting up the words one at a time.

National Curriculum Links for Key Stage 2

Literacy
En3
Writing
7 and 10
ICT
1b
Numeracy
Ma4) 1e and H

TOPIC LINKS

Literature
What Makes a Good Story
Favourite Stories
Statistics
Percentages

Journey into Space

You will need:
Microsoft Word
Access to books about space
Internet access

The Task

Can you write a short story describing a journey in a spacecraft from Earth to Mars?

Take a look at some books about space. What would it be like to travel to another planet and what would you find once you land?

If you have access to the internet you can browse the NASA website to see what space looks like, or go to the planetarium site and research the planets.

First you will need to adapt your computer in preparation for the journey.

Here's how to do it.

Click on Start, then settings and then select 'Control Panel'. Once in control panel click and open Display.

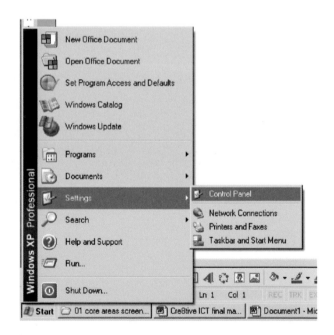

Now select 'Appearance' from 'Display Properties'.

Now select 'Windows Classic Style' and 'High Contrast Black' from the menu.

Wow! It's all turned black. Now you can begin your story!

Notes for Parents and Teachers

Children find space and sci-fi stories fascinating and they will be taught about it at some stage of their primary education. This is a simple but very effective way of getting children into the mood for writing. It is equally appropriate for reluctant writers and for the more able.

These are some great links:

NASA *www.nasa.gov*
Kennedy space center *www.ksc.nasa.gov*
London Planetarium *www.madame-tussauds.com*
European Space Agency *www.esrin.esa.it*
British National Space Centre *www.bnsc.gov.uk*
Patrick Moore (The Sky at Night) *www.bbc.co.uk*

TOPIC LINKS

Creative Writing
Space
Science Fiction
Genre

Humanities and science: Back to the future... forward into history

In these activities we bring ICT skills to bear on themes and concepts in the humanities and science in a way that might not at first be obvious. Historical and scientific concepts are used as departure points for the innovative application of 'Word' programs. Basic core ICT skills can be applied to making fun and informative outcomes which extend and develop children's deeper understanding of the themes covered.

Super Solar System

You will need: Microsoft Word and access to information about the Solar System.

As part of your science work in school, or perhaps just because you are interested, you will need to know the composition of the Solar System. After all, this does occur as a science attainment target and, what's more, it's fun!

You can make your own graphical representation of the Solar System simply by using 'Word', 'AutoShapes' 'Fill Colour' and 'WordArt'.

The Task

You simply use the 'Oval' facility in 'AutoShapes' to create your planets. Remember to try to keep them to proportional sizes (Jupiter is much bigger than Mercury, for example).

Oval Facility

If you research the diameters of each planet you can estimate how much bigger or smaller they are than each other. For example Venus has a diameter of 12,104 km and Earth has a diameter of 12,756 km, so they would be about the same. Mars has a diameter of 6,187 km so how much smaller, approximately, is the diameter of Mars compared to Earth and Venus? You can find this information on a number of websites. We have found these two to be pretty good: *www.dustbunny.com* and *www.esse.ou.edu*

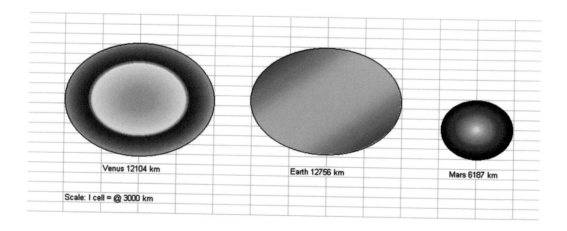

Venus 12104 km   Earth 12756 km   Mars 6187 km

Scale: I cell = @ 3000 km

Using these websites will also help you match the colours accurately. You colour your planets by going to the 'Fill Colour' toolbar

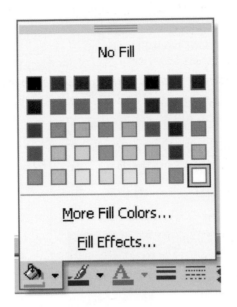

Better still, go to 'Fill Effects' on the bottom of 'Fill Colour'. It is good fun to experiment with the different 'Gradients' and 'Textures'. Just click on 'Texture' to see the options.

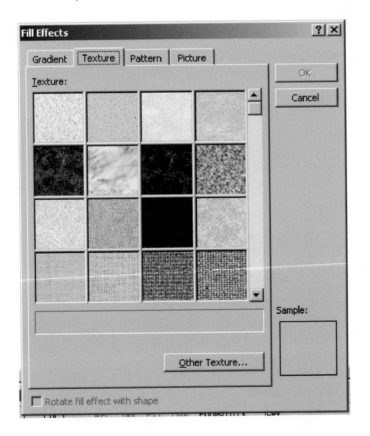

Click on 'Gradients' and then colours to see the varieties of colours you can mix. Go to 'Shading Styles' to see how they can be blended.

Once you have created your planets you can label them through 'WordArt'.

WordArt

Stars can be made via 'Stars and Banners' in 'AutoShapes' and you could make the sun in this way if you wanted to, because we all know that the sun is really a star.

To create the black space go to 'Format' on the top toolbar and click 'Background'.

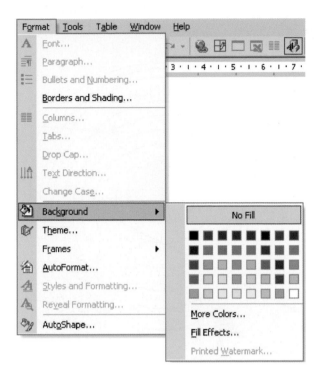

Challenge

If you want to create an asteroid belt then 'Copy and Paste' your Solar System into 'Paint' and use the 'Spray' facility to give the effect of an asteriod belt (see below).

You could now go on to invent your own imaginary galaxies and 'Copy and Paste' them into the comic ideas that are in the section on Roy Lichtenstein.

Use the same techniques above to create a planet with a moon. 'Copy and Paste' the moon in different positions then go into 'Undo' and click it again and again to create a moving picture.

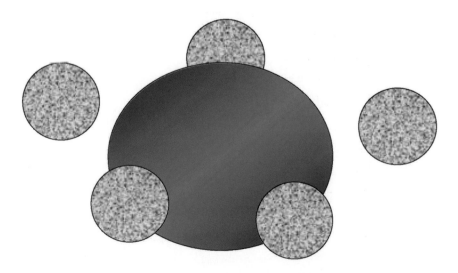

Look at the illustration below. Scott and Harrison decided they wanted to extend the activity to show the orbits of the planets. After researching the topic they created the example below. Can you work out how they did it?

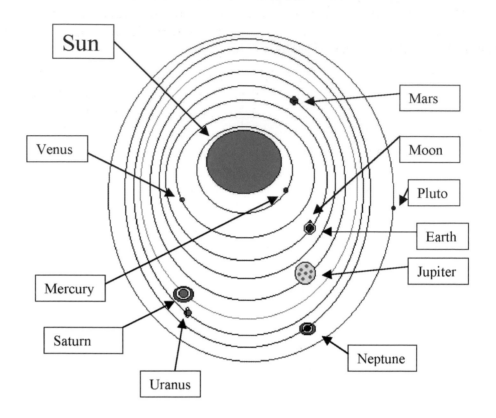

Notes for Parents and Teachers

This is a great activity that allows children to familiarise themselves with the composition of the Solar System and fulfils the National Curriculum requirement for 'Earth and Space'. It is thus a good introduction to astronomy, and a quite sophisticated use of various toolbars. It also allows for the manipulation of a number of Microsoft programs.

The task also gives an opportunity for children to develop a sense of scale, albeit by eye rather than by calculation – though if they research the diameters of planets then computational skills can be brought into play. It is useful for familiarising the children with surfing the internet to look for specific statistical data, and provides a fun activity as part of a small project on space. We have used it as a cross-curricular link to creative writing where the focus has been on stories and poems about space (see the 'nice negatives' unit). Remember that there have been some very famous space stories and if children are looking at science fiction as a genre then this can be linked to that as well. The task can also be used in conjunction with the next unit on the Solar System which uses Excel.

National Curriculum Links for Key Stage 2

Science
Sc4) 4a and 4b

TOPIC LINKS

Sci-Fi
Space
Space Travel
Solar System
Big Numbers

Solar System to Scale

You will need: Microsoft Excel and some statistical information about the distances between the planets of the Solar System. This is a follow up activity to 'Super Solar System'.

If you want to add to your knowledge on the Solar System and practise your numeracy skills with some pretty big numbers then here is a great idea using Excel.

The Task

Go to Excel. You get there through clicking on 'Start', 'Programs' and then click on 'Microsoft Excel'.

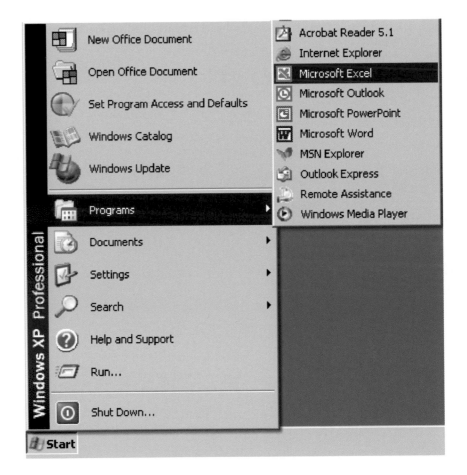

You will notice that the sheet is divided into little rectangles called 'cells'.

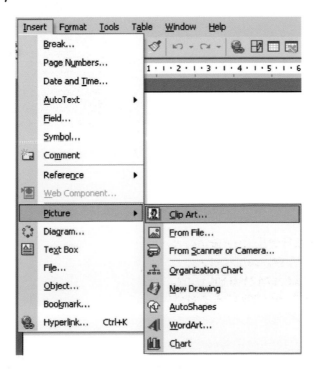

Click on any cell to type in it. This works the same as in Word. If you want to change a spelling, delete things or move them around you can.

Using the oval facility from 'AutoShapes', create your planets and colour them appropriately using 'Fill Color' and 'Fill Effects'. Go to the instructions on 'Super Solar System' if you cannot remember how to use them.

You could go to 'Insert' on the toolbar at the top of the window and see if there are some planets on 'Clip Art' that you could put in. When the 'Clip Art' window appears you can look under either 'Clip Art' or 'Images'. Click on the image you want and then click on 'Insert'. The image will be transferred to your work.

You could decorate it by using star shapes from 'AutoShapes' if you wanted to.

The scale you choose is up to you and depends on how big you want your Solar System to be.

We think the best way to create the scale is to make each cell equal to a certain distance. For example, one cell = 15,000,000 miles. You can print off more than one page so you could make it pretty big. These two websites are pretty good for giving you the statistical information you need: *www.dustbunny.com* and *www.esse.ou.edu*. There are others and a great website to check out is the NASA website. Just put NASA into your search engine and follow the links.

Challenge

If you are feeling really clever you could put in all the different moons of the different planets to scale and if you are feeling really, really clever then you could try and do the planets to scale as well. What kind of mathematical information are you going to need to do that?

Notes for Parents and Teachers

This task follows on from 'Super Solar System' and provides an opportunity for children to increase their knowledge of the Solar System beyond the expectations of the National Curriculum. It also gives them the opportunity to practise their skills of approximation and scale.

Best done as a class activity in the ICT suite, this activity is a novel way to introduce 'Excel' as more than just a data-handling program. It allows pupils to become familiar with the properties of 'Excel' and combine their existing 'Word' skills with the program. It gives pupils the opportunity to develop their skills of approximation and scale using pretty large numbers and the challenges are designed to stretch the powers of the more able mathematicians.

National Curriculum Links for Key Stage 2

Science
Sc4) 4a and 4b
ICT
2a

TOPIC LINKS

Sci-Fi
Space
Space Travel
Solar System
Big Numbers
Proportion
Ratio

Illuminated Letters

You will need: Microsoft Word and information on, and examples of, illuminated letters.

When you do history in school, you will certainly come across the Tudors and Stuarts. Part of your work may well focus on the beautiful manuscripts that were produced at this time. You will also discover that the Anglo-Saxon monks created some of the earliest illuminated manuscripts. These manuscripts were very intricate and beautifully coloured and decorated. They were mainly created by monks who made them as perfect as they could in order to show their love and devotion to God. The monks were very good at extracting natural dyes from plants and were able to make many rich and vivid inks. This task will show you how to make an illuminated letter like these examples from history.

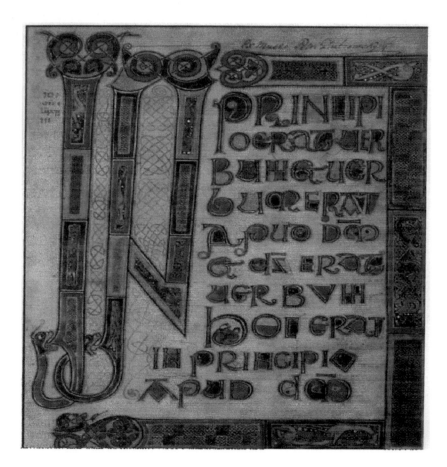

Emme, Year 7

The Task

You can start designing your illuminated letters by giving them a frame using 'Text Box'. Your research will give you some inspiration. Go to the 'AutoShapes' toolbar and choose 'Text Box'. 'Text Box' works the same way as the 'Rectangle' facility. Click the icon and then left-click on the mouse on the screen and create your square.

You will see the cursor flashing in the box. That is where you can type your letter. Don't type it yet.

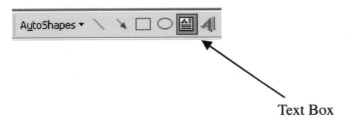

Text Box

You can fill the inside of the 'Text Box' frame by choosing colours or designs from 'Fill Colour'. You can change the colours and thickness of the edges by using 'Line Style' and 'Line Colour'. They are on the bottom toolbar.

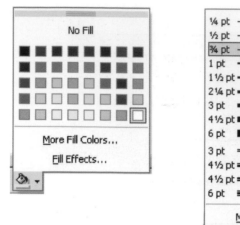

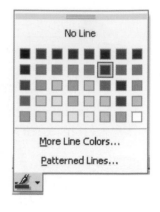

Here is a simple example: we used 'Fill Effects' for the inside and 'Line Style' and 'Line Colour' to make the edge a thick blue line.

Next you need to choose a suitable font. There are loads to choose from and it will take some browsing. To see all the font options click on 'Format' on the top toolbar. The font option will appear at the top. Click on that and the font window will appear. You can play around with 'Style', 'Size' and 'Effects' until the letter looks the way you want it to. You can see the changes in the 'Preview' window.

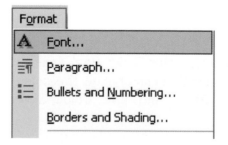

Once you are happy with your letter, you can start thinking about how you can make your design more elaborate. You can experiment with all the facilities in 'AutoShapes'. You can overlay it with other smaller shapes or decorate it with lines.

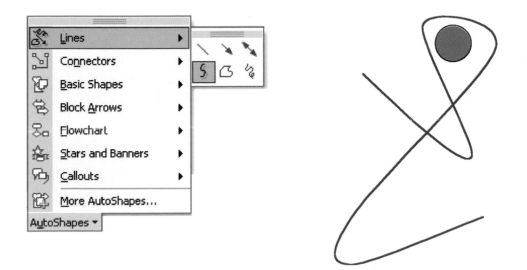

You can make your writing look like an ancient manuscript by writing in columns. Go to 'Format' on the top toolbar and click on 'Columns' then choose the layout you want. We think splitting the page down the middle is the most authentic. While you are in 'Format', use 'Borders and Shading' to put a border around your work.

Format	
A	Font...
	Paragraph...
	Bullets and Numbering...
	Borders and Shading...
	Columns...

✎ Notes for Parents and Teachers

This is an activity that really allows children to research an aspect of history and trace its development. There are some superb examples of manuscripts across history, one of the most magnificent being 'The Book of Kells' in the library at Trinity College Dublin.

In the classroom this is a great activity to use with a number of history topics. It is an excellent one to research on the internet as there are thousands of sites devoted to the topic. Perhaps two of the best are the websites belonging to the Bodleian Library Oxford and the library of Trinity College Dublin. Children are able to study the writing and printing techniques of historical eras and emulate them with the most sophisticated technology currently available to humankind. You can print them off on coloured paper for extra authenticity. We have found that children are also very keen to extend and develop this task by creating their own dyes, inks and quills and making freehand versions of their computer generated art. Placing the two mediums side by side can make a stunning and informative display. It also provides an opportunity to get to know other aspects of Word and use them creatively.

National Curriculum Links for Key Stage 2

History
1a, 1b, 2d and 4b
ICT
5c and 2a

TOPIC LINKS

Manuscripts
Printing
Calligraphy
Religion
Monks
Saxons
Tudors
Bible

Fabulous Family Trees

You will need: Microsoft Excel and information on the family lineage you are studying. An example of a family tree that you can use as a model would be helpful. You will need to know how to use Word.

Look at the example diagram at the end of the task to see an example of a family tree. This is a great idea to help you with your history. You might be studying a certain period of history or you might need to trace the lineage of an overseas dynasty or royal family. In Key Stage 2 you will certainly look at Vikings, Saxon and Tudor kings and queens or you might be doing a project on your own family. Either way this is a great way to start. If you are doing your own family, speaking to grandparents and aunts and uncles is a great way to start gathering information.

The Task

Go to Excel. You get there through 'Start', 'Programs' and then clicking on 'Microsoft Excel'.

You will notice that the sheet is divided into little rectangles called 'cells'.

Click on any cell to type in it. This works in exactly the same way as Word. If you want to change a spelling, delete things or move them around you can.

You need to start at the top of the tree with the oldest people first. Because the tree spreads out from the top you will have to estimate your starting point. It won't be next to the left-hand margin. Try starting in cell H3 to begin with. Type in it, don't worry if your typing goes over more than one cell.

You can draw the arrows, in exactly the same way as you do in Word. Remember, they are part of the 'AutoShapes' toolbar at the bottom of the screen. Don't make the arrows too long. Lead them to a cell and type your information in that cell. To make everything look really neat and tidy leave an equal number of cells between each entry.

If you want to, you can go to 'Insert' and put in some 'Clip Art' to make your tree look really cool. 'Insert' is on the toolbar at the top of your screen. Browse through the categories for images that suit your family tree.

In order to help you lay your family tree out properly you will need to use 'Print Preview'. Remember that you find it under 'File' on the top toolbar. It works in exactly the same way as it does in Word.

When you print your family tree, you won't see the cells so everything looks really neat and tidy.

Once you have printed it you can also add your own illustrations by hand if you want to.

Challenge

If you are feeling really clever you can scan images from other sources into your family tree, or if you are doing your own family tree, take digital pictures of your family members. You can scan in images from family photographs as well.

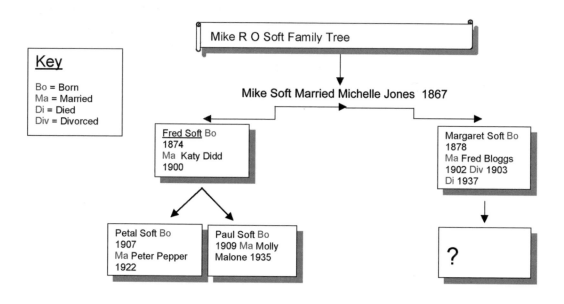

Mike R O Soft Family Tree

Key

Bo = Born
Ma = Married
Di = Died
Div = Divorced

Mike Soft Married Michelle Jones 1867

Fred Soft Bo 1874
Ma Katy Didd 1900

Margaret Soft Bo 1878
Ma Fred Bloggs 1902 Div 1903
Di 1937

Petal Soft Bo 1907
Ma Peter Pepper 1922

Paul Soft Bo 1909 Ma Molly Malone 1935

?

Notes for Parents and Teachers

This is a fun exercise that encourages a number of historical enquiry skills, helps to provide a longitudinal view of history, and uses a number of ICT skills. If children are interested in history, then this is an exercise for them. The challenges at the end are particularly good for stretching the more able.

In the classroom this could be used as an ongoing activity where pairs or small groups of children take it in turns to make contributions to a large-scale presentation. Equally, it can be used as an individual activity if children are engaged in researching and presenting their own family tree. It does require research beforehand as the children have to be armed with the historical data they need.

The task is also developmental as the children need to have consolidated their skills in Word before moving onto Excel. An important point for teachers to note is that the 'AutoShapes' toolbar might not appear at the bottom of the Excel page. Simply go to 'View' on the top toolbar, click on 'Toolbars' and then click on 'Drawing'. The toolbar will automatically appear. There is also a degree of trial and error involved as far as the layout goes. Family trees do get wider as they develop and children may find that they have to move things around. Deleting and moving is done in exactly the same way as it is in Word. Patience and planning are prerequisites for this task.

National Curriculum Links for KS2

History
1a, 1b and 2d
Historical Enquiry
4b and 5c

TOPIC LINKS

Dynasties
Autobiography
Life Cycles
Families
My Family
Chronology
Genealogy

Parallel Time Lines

You will need: Microsoft Excel and chronological information on different historical eras.

Look at the example at the end of the task to see how we have started a parallel time line of our own. This is a great idea to help you with your history. It can show you what was going on in different places at the same time in history. For example, do you know what was going on in other parts of the world when the Vikings were invading Britain?

If you want to you could use this task to plot a time line of your own life. You could start with a time line of your life and then make parallel lines for things that have occurred as you have got older. For example, when Simon was 11 England won the World Cup in football (can you work out how old Simon is now?). Adam in Year 6 has made a time line of some of the significant events in his life. Will took a slightly different approach but they both work. Which style are you going to do yours in?

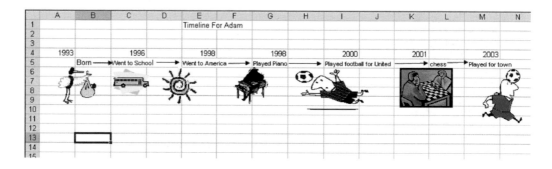

Adam, Year 6

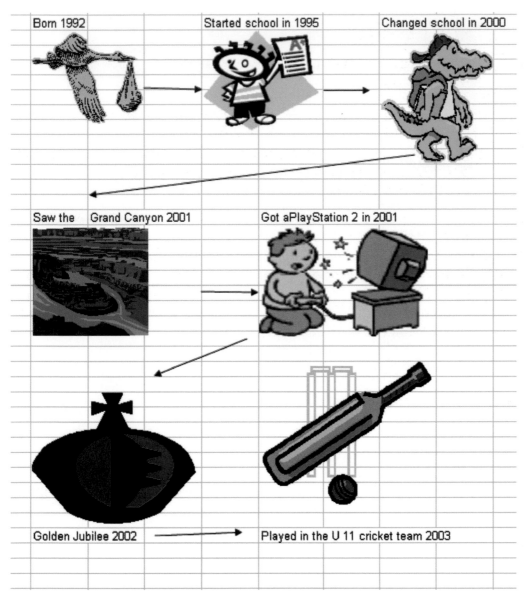

Born 1992

Started school in 1995

Changed school in 2000

Saw the Grand Canyon 2001

Got aPlayStation 2 in 2001

Golden Jubilee 2002

Played in the U 11 cricket team 2003

Will, Year 6

The Task

Go to Excel. You get there by clicking on 'Start', 'Programs' and then 'Microsoft Excel'.

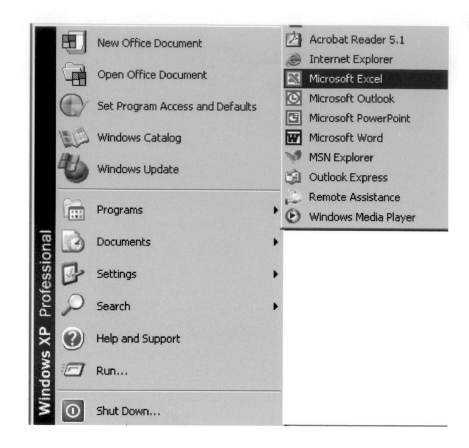

You will notice that the sheet is divided into little rectangles called 'cells'.

Click on any cell to type in it. This works in exactly the same way as Word. If you want to change a spelling, delete things or move them around you can. You can add arrows, in exactly the same way as you do with Word. Remember, they are part of the 'AutoShapes' toolbar at the bottom of the screen.

You will notice that we have also gone to 'Insert' and put in some 'Clip Art' to make it look really cool. 'Insert' is on the toolbar at the top of your screen. Browse through the categories for images that suit your time line.

The great thing about Excel is that you can go on for ages. If you are doing a long time line (maybe you could make it stretch around the classroom) then go to 'File' then go to 'Page Setup' then go to 'Paper Size' and change the orientation to 'Landscape'. There is a story called 'The Roman Beanfeast' where one of the children makes a really long time line – it's a good story. Look for it in your library.

When you print your time line off you won't see the cells, so everything looks really neat and tidy.

Once you have printed it you can add your own illustrations by hand if you want to.

If you are feeling really clever you can scan images from other sources onto your time line, or take a digital picture of yourself dressed up as a famous historical figure and scan that into your time line. By doing that you can really become part of history.

Challenge

If you plot your own life as a time line you could stick/scan/draw in some of your favourite and important times like photographs of holidays, birthdays and other important events.

	Parallel Time Lines			
	7000 BC	5000 BC	3000 BC	1000 BC
EUROPE	First farming in Greece on Aegean coast	Farming in N'ern Europe and Britain		Etruscans arrive in Italy
ASIA	Rice cultivation in China		1st Agricultural settlements	Indo Aryan settlements on Ganges plain
AFRICA	Evidence of work with copper		Development of major cities in Sumer	Emergence of Israelite kingdom

✍ Notes for Parents and Teachers

This is a fun exercise that encourages a number of historical enquiry skills, helps to provide a comparative historical overview and uses a number of ICT skills. If children are interested in history, then this is an exercise for them. The challenge at the end is particularly good for stretching the more able.

In the classroom this could be used as an ongoing activity where pairs or small groups of children take it in turns to make contributions to a large-scale presentation. Equally, it can be used as an individual activity or an ICT suite task. It does require research beforehand as the children have to be armed with the historical data they need.

The task is also developmental, as the children need to have consolidated their skills in Word before moving onto Excel. An important point for teachers to note is that the AutoShapes toolbar might not appear at the bottom of the Excel page. Simply go to 'View' on the top toolbar, click on 'Toolbars' and then click on 'Drawing'. The toolbar will automatically appear.

National Curriculum Links for Key Stage 2

History
1a, 1b and 2d
Historical Enquiry
4b and 5c

TOPIC LINKS

Comparative History
Chronology
Autobiography
Families
My Family
Ancient History
Civilisations
Religions

CHAPTER 3

Art: Get the picture?

The following activities and ideas combine creative use of Word with images of famous works of art as a departure point for children's own artwork. Some units also bring in aspects of maths as an additional context within which art can be created and understood. All the activities help to develop a deeper understanding of art and of how the art tools in Word can be utilised to create original work. The following websites all provide additional links for each activity: *www.nationalgallery.org.uk, www.tate.org.uk, www.npg.si.edu, www.hayward-gallery.org.uk.*

Roaring Roy Lichtenstein

You will need: Microsoft Word and access to information about the artist Roy Lichtenstein.

The Task

Check out the artwork of Roy Lichtenstein on CD-ROM, on the internet (*www.lichtensteinfoundation.org*) or at your local library. He was very well known for his large scale 'Comic Book' style (see the picture above). His artwork is called 'Pop Art'. What can you find out about this?

Here are two examples of artwork created by a child in year 6:

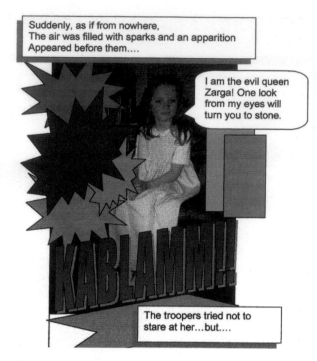

Emme, Year 6

In this example Emme has taken an action image of herself using a digital camera and downloaded it into Word. She used 'Cut and Paste' to import the image into a comic frame she had already created and added speech bubbles and text, using the steps described below.

You can create your own Lichtenstein style art by using Word, 'Text Box', 'Paint', 'WordArt' and 'Clip Art'. Here's how it's done...

Click on 'Text Box' to create a frame for your picture. (Windows XP users should create a text box outside of the computer generated frame.) Click on your document and drag the cursor to make your frame the size you want.

Here's how you choose a background colour for your frame by going to 'Fill Colour'.

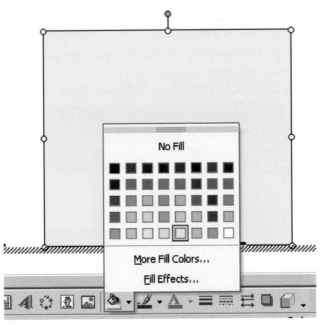

This is the 'Fill Colour' icon. I've chosen a light turquoise for my background.

To change the look of your background you need to use 'Fill Effects'. Click on the arrow by the 'Fill Colour' icon and then click on 'Fill Effects'. Play around with the options and see what different art effects you can get!

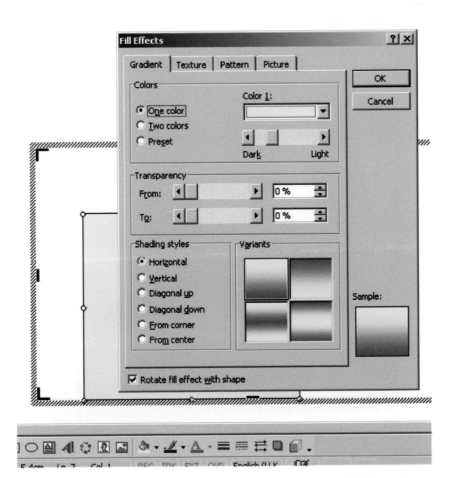

Now it's time to add a picture. Click on your text box to select it then click on 'Insert' on the main toolbar, then 'Picture', then 'Clip Art' and browse for a character or a theme. Once you have chosen, click on 'Insert'. The picture should appear inside your frame.

If you want to change the picture or the frame, simply select the picture by clicking on it then press the delete button.

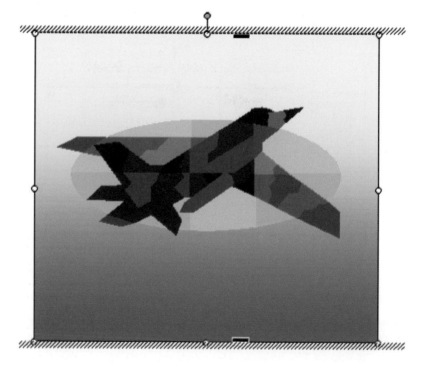

To insert speech bubbles go back to 'AutoShapes' and use 'Callouts'. You will see a little yellow diamond on the point of the bubble that will lead to the character's mouth. Just click on it and drag it to where you want it to go. You can write inside the bubble.

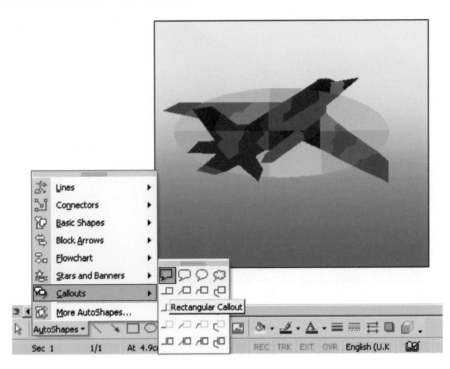

By clicking on 'WordArt' you can now pick a comic book style for your writing.

Again, click and drag it to where you want it to go.

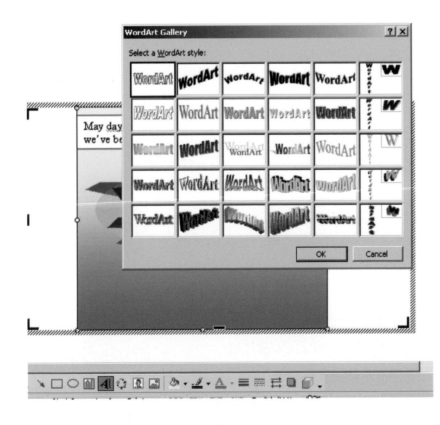

Challenge

Now you have your very own work of art in the style of Lichtenstein! Can you create a series of pictures and make your own comic strip?

✍ Notes for Parents and Teachers

This is a great activity that introduces one of the pioneers of modern art who was a massive influence on the comic book culture. Just as importantly, it allows for quite sophisticated manipulation of Microsoft Word that serves as a great introduction to more advanced publishing program. The activity can bring a new dimension to structure in story writing and support the development of ideas. It can inspire reluctant writers, while the more able writers can attempt to create a number of comic strips to make a short story.

Roy Lichtenstein is an American artist who lived from 1923–1997. His work based on comic strips began around 1960, when one day he attempted to copy a cartoon. Between 1961 and 1965 Lichtenstein used images ranging from advertising to common objects. They fall into three main groups – love and romance, science fiction, and war and violence. In 1964 an article appeared in Life Magazine posing the question: Is He the Worst Artist in the U.S? Some critics felt that this was indeed true as his work was everyday and mundane, whilst others felt that his work was fascinating. The Roy Lichtenstein Foundation (*www.lichtensteinfoundation*) provides a great deal of background information on the artist.

There are a number of ways this activity can be used:

- As a way of looking at how text is changed depending on the purpose of the text and the intended audience. Why is a comic different to a book? Who might read a comic?
- As a means of teaching the ICT knowledge, skills and understanding needed to develop the children's ability.
- As a discussion about the artist and art generally. Was he a bad artist? What makes a good artist? Does art have to be representational to be good?

National Curriculum Links for Key Stage 2

This activity covers:

English
Reading En2, Writing En3, Breadth of Study 9a
Art
3a, 4c, 5a
ICT
2a, 3b, 4a, 4b, and 4c

TOPIC LINKS

Pop Art
American Art
Comics
Cartoons
Creative Writing
Publishing
Graphic Design

Virtual Picasso

Microsoft Word and access to information about Picasso.

Sculpture: the art of making shapes in 3-D, often by chiselling stone, carving wood, modelling clay, casting metal, etc.

The Guitar Player (1910) by Pablo Picasso

The Task

Above is an example of a cubist painting by Picasso. It is made from many different mathematical shapes. One shape Picasso used a lot was the cube, and this style of painting was called 'Cubism'. In this painting, Picasso tries to show different viewpoints in one painting. Can you see how he did it?

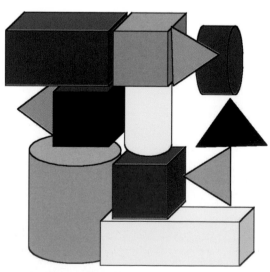

Anthony, Year 5

You can design your own virtual sculpture based on a cubist painting, by using 'AutoShapes', arranging them, then filling them with colour. Then make it for real! Here's how to do it...

Click on 'AutoShapes', and then select a 3-D shape from 'Basic Shapes'. Click and drag to re-size it.

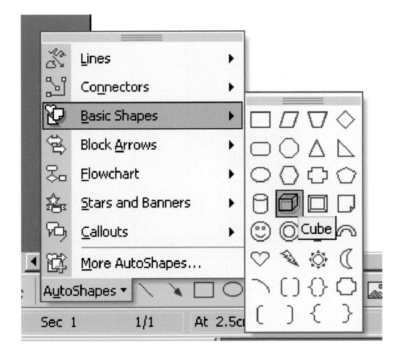

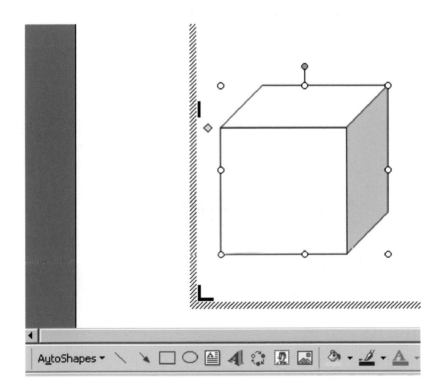

The tiny circles around the shape tell the computer that this is the shape you want to work on (in Windows 98 these are squares instead of circles).

Now add some more shapes – have fun experimenting!

By selecting 'Order' you can change the position of your shape, and hide it behind or in front of another shape. To do this right-click on the shape to bring up the menu.

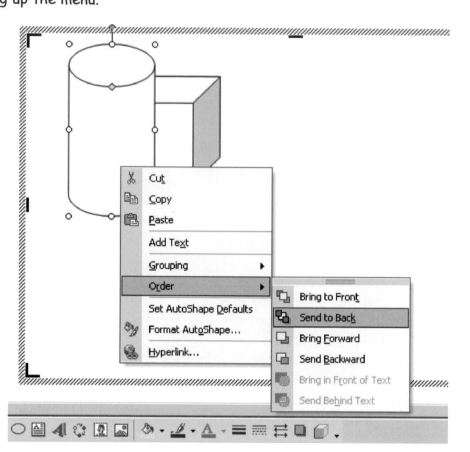

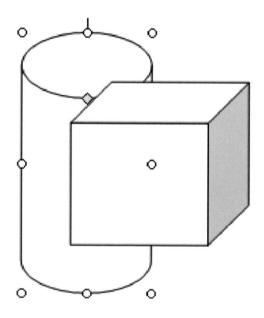

Here I have moved the cylinder behind the cube.

Keep building up your virtual sculpture using more shapes...

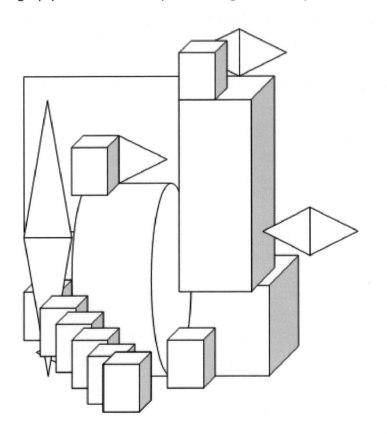

Once you are happy with your virtual sculpture you can add colour. Just click on the shape you want to colour, and then click on the 'Fill Colour' icon.

Here I have selected the drum shape and I am going to colour it orange.

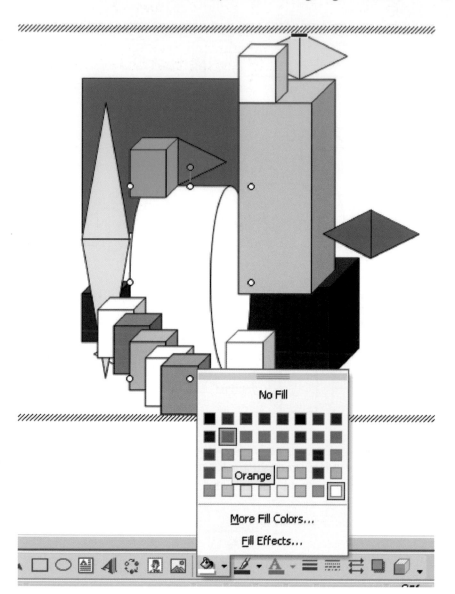

Challenge

Once your virtual sculpture is completed you can photocopy onto card the different nets of shapes (you will find these at the back of this book under resources), and make your very own cubist sculpture.

✍ Notes for Parents and Teachers

This is an unusual way of using simple computer aided design. It introduces children to the idea of planning out an idea before actually making it, using a computer. It also gives them a simple understanding of cubism and how the work of the cubists is predominantly made up of mathematical shapes.

Picasso was a Spanish artist who lived from 1881 to 1973. As he grew up his father taught him art. Picasso went through a number of styles and influences before he and George Braque developed Cubism. During his Blue period, 1901–1904, he would use much blue in his paintings often using images of down-and-outs. The Rose period followed and he used a lighter palette made up of pinks, using images of circus performers. One of Picasso's most famous works 'Guernica' 1937, was painted for the International World Fair. The Spanish Republic was under siege at the time and urged Picasso to paint something that showed the horror of the fascists. Guernica was a small Spanish village in which over a thousand villagers died from a Nazi aerial bombardment. The website *www.artchive.com* has links to his work from different periods of his life.

Picasso described Cubism as 'an art dealing primarily with forms'. In my own classroom practice I've used this idea as part of a maths investigation. The focus of the lesson was to revise the names of 2-D shapes. I first asked the class to name as many 2-D shapes as they could think of. Next they looked at a painting by Picasso, identifying and recording the frequency and type of different shapes. For the plenary we looked to see if there was a pattern to the frequency and type of shapes he used – were cubes really the most dominant shape?

National Curriculum Links for Key Stage 2

This activity covers:

Art
4c and 5b
ICT
2a

TOPIC LINKS

Picasso
Modern Art
Sculpture
Shape and Space
3-D Shape
Volume
Cubism
Cubists
Spanish Civil War

Excellent Escher

You will need: Microsoft Word or any other word processing program, access to information about Escher and examples of his work.

The Task

Look at the picture below.

'Up and Down' (1947) by Escher
© 2004 The M. C. Escher Company, Baarn, Holland

What do you notice? Is this possible in the real world? Escher's pictures played around with perspective to create confusing images.

Perspective: the illusion of 3-D space on a flat 2-D surface.

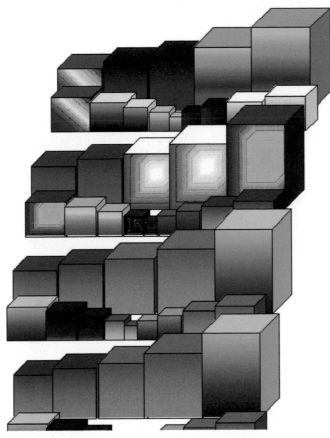

Katie and Laura, Year 4

Can you find out more about the use of perspective in art? Can you see how Escher uses it in very unusual ways?

You can make your own art with a zany perspective. Here's how it's done...

Click on 'AutoShapes', then select a 2-D shape from 'Basic Shapes'.

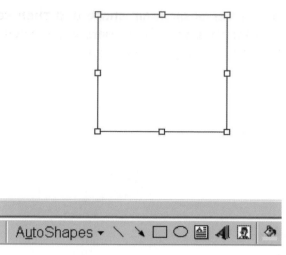

To make your artwork look 3-D you can use the '3-D Settings'. To do this click on to your square shape, select the '3-D Settings' icon and choose an effect.

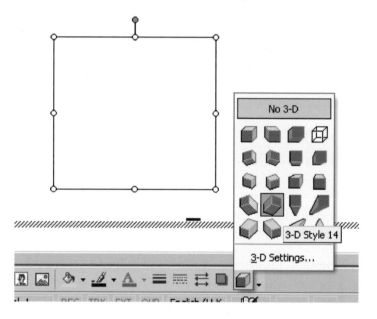

To move and rotate your cuboid shapes you need to use the 'Free Rotate' facility so that you can start to play with the perspective.

Windows XP users should click and hold on the green circle to rotate your cuboid.

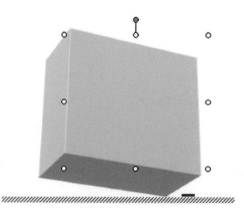

Windows 98 users should click on their shape and then select the 'Free Rotate' icon from the 'Draw' toolbar. Once the green circles have appeared, click and drag one of them to rotate your shape.

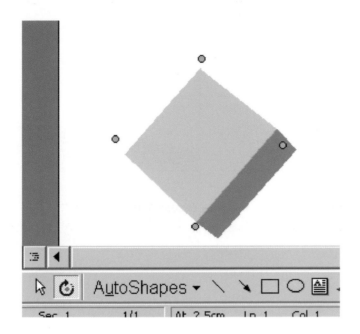

You can experiment with the colours of the cubes and art effects like this:

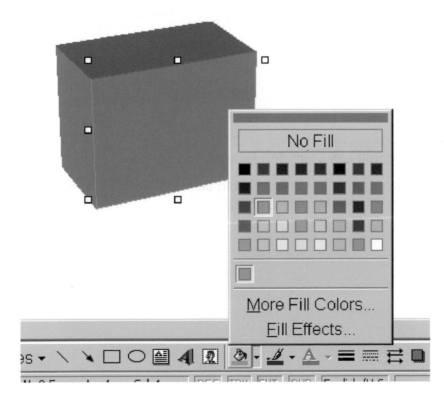

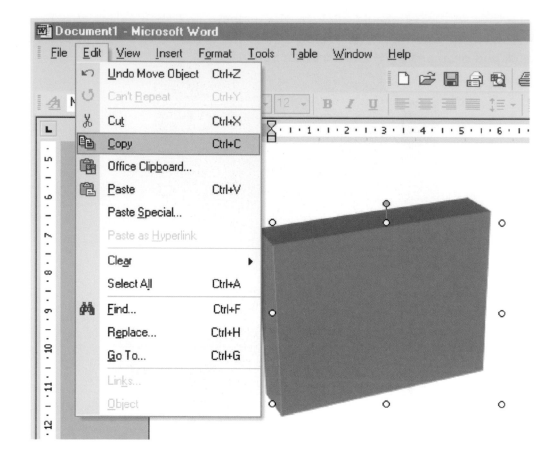

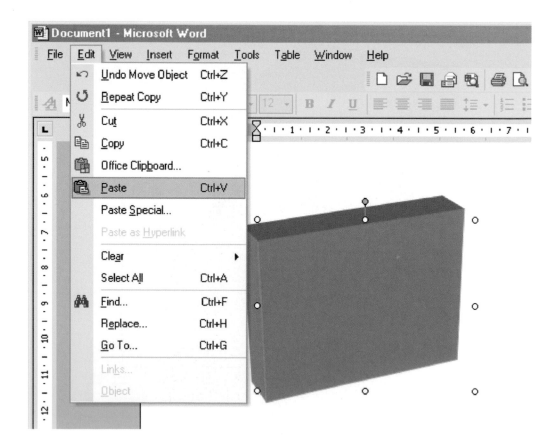

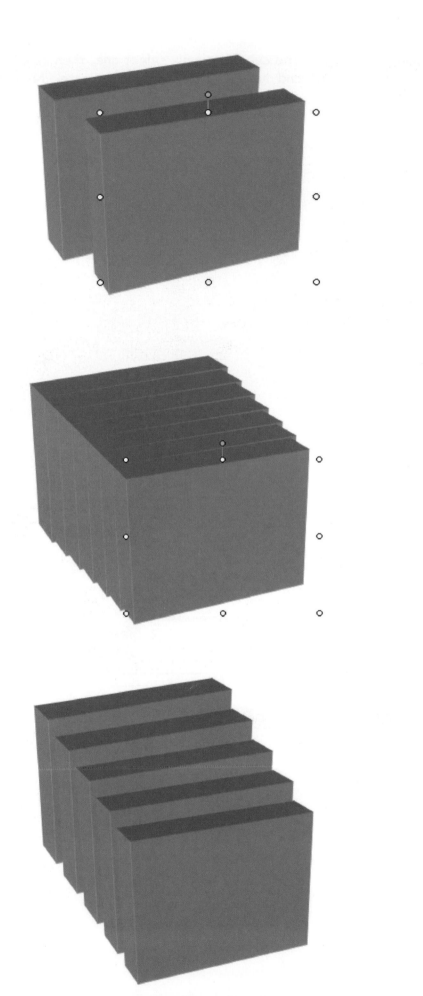

To play around with the cuboids simply select one, then select 'Edit' from the top menu bar and select 'Copy' and then 'Paste'. Now repeat the process.

✍ Notes for Parents and Teachers

This activity allows children to get to know the work of a great artist and to engage in a problem solving activity that requires reasoning and investigation: how do you get the cubes to look as though they are disappearing away from you?

Escher was a Dutch artist who lived from 1898 to 1972. During his lifetime he made hundreds of woodcuts, wood engravings and lithographs. He also illustrated books, murals and postage stamps. He is most famous for his pictures depicting spatial illusions of impossible spaces and tessellating patterns. The website *www.mcescher.com* is a good source of information and has a free downloadable Escher puzzle. For a good range of downloadable Escher pictures visit the California State University website, *www.cs.unc.edu/~davemc/Pic/Escher*.

This is a great way of discovering what you can do using the 'AutoShapes' toolbar. It can provide an imaginative introduction to a number of mathematical concepts such as area, volume and the properties of shapes. It is also a good introduction to the concept of perspective. The activity could be integrated as an extension activity into numeracy work on shape and space.

Alternatively, it could be used as it is as a means of developing ICT skills in an art context. To develop the perspective effect takes a little time and it would be worth trying this out on your own before introducing it to children. Once the children get the hang of it they get a real sense of achievement. Above all it is fun!

National Curriculum Links for Key Stage 2

This activity covers:

Numeracy
Ma3) 1, 2 and 3
Art
4a, 4b and 5c
ICT
2a

TOPIC LINKS

Perspective
Golden Mean
Optical Illusion
Space and Shape
3-D Shapes
Tessellation

Dooby Dooby Dürer

You will need: Microsoft Word and access to information on the artist Albrecht Dürer.

This is a cool way to find out about an influential artist and the techniques he pioneered.

The Task

Find out about Albrecht Dürer on CD-ROM, the internet or your local library.

'Rhinoceros' (1515) by Dürer
Reproduced by permission of the St Bride Printing Library

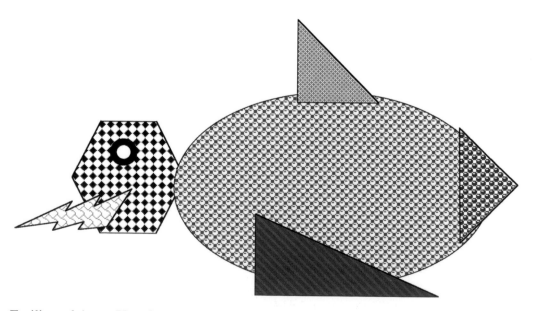

Emilie and Anna, Year 3

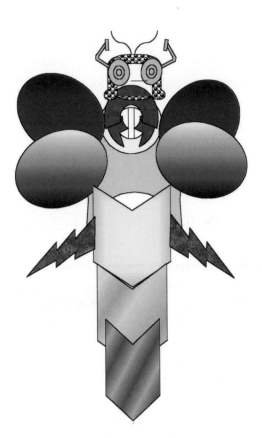

Adam, Year 6

Wasn't Dürer brilliant at using line and shading? Just look at the variety of shapes and techniques he used. The illustrations above have been done by pupils who have been inspired by Dürer.

Create a creature of your own – it could be an animal or a mythical creature. You'll be using 'Line' and 'AutoShapes'. Here's how to do it . . .

You can build up your picture by simply using lines . . .

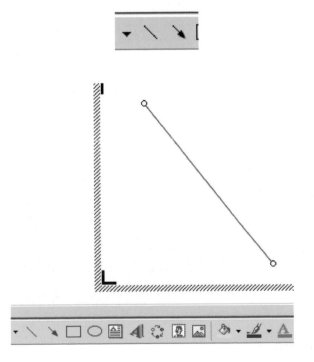

...and 'Basic Shapes'.

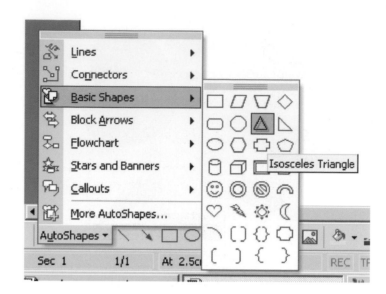

I decided to make a fish!

To create the 'Dürer' type effect, click on part of your drawing, then click on 'Fill Colour' and then 'Fill Effects', and choose a pattern of your choice.

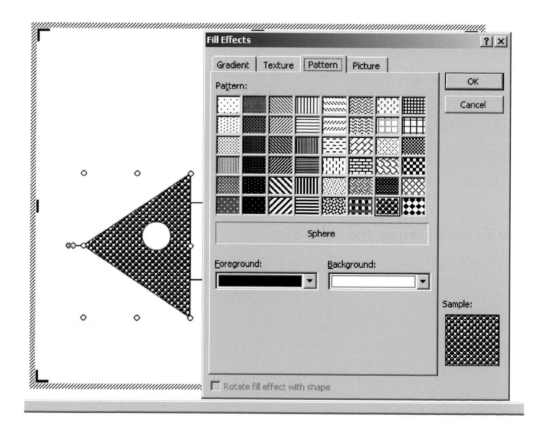

By selecting a shape, then clicking on to 'More Lines', the thickness of the line can be changed.

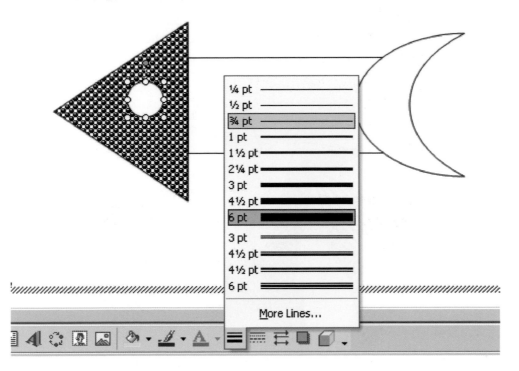

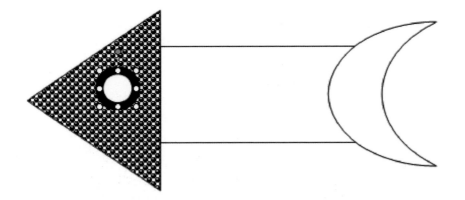

Here I have thickened the fish's eye.

And here's my finished fish.

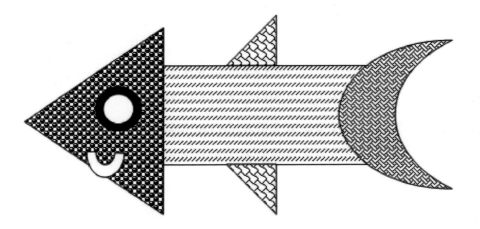

Challenge

You can create a great effect by printing out the basic outline of your creature. Colour some of it in by hand, and use a collage of newspaper clippings to fill in other parts. Then, if you scan the image back in to the computer, you can finish it off with 'Fill Effects'.

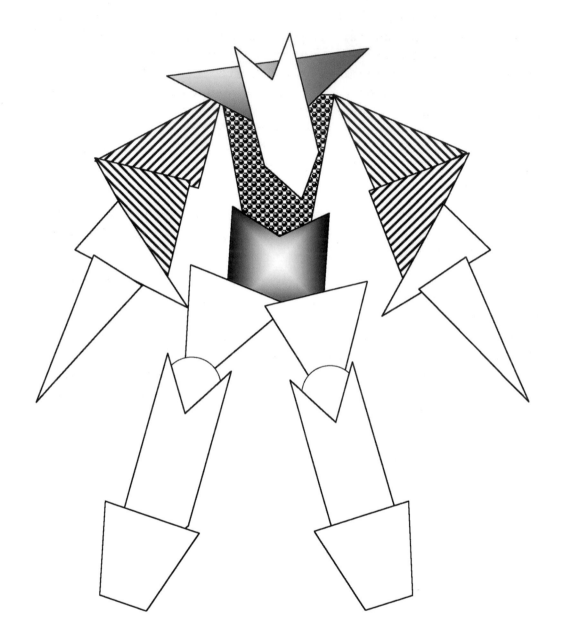

✍ Notes for Parents and Teachers

This is a great way to introduce children to influential artists of the last millennium and the visual and tactile elements of artwork. The children will develop awareness that there can be many elements to a picture, not just line. These include tone, shape, pattern, form and space.

Dürer was a German artist who lived from 1471 to 1528. His father was a goldsmith and Dürer trained as a draughtsman in his father's workshop. The self-portrait he completed in 1484 when he was only 13 demonstrates his early mastery over his chosen medium. To continue his training his father arranged an apprenticeship with an artist called Michael Wolgumut. During his lifetime he painted the rich and famous, including kings and important government officials. For a time he worked for the Holy Roman emperor Maximillian I, and one of his projects was to produce some drawings for the Emperor's prayer book. For more information on Dürer, explore the artchive website *www.artchive.com* and WebMuseum Paris at *www.sunsite.unc.edu*

This activity, creating a computer-generated character, opens up all sorts of possibilities for creative writing. Children can give the character a whole history and use it as a character in their creative writing.

I've used this activity in art lessons to introduce the vocabulary 'line', 'shape', 'pattern' and 'tone'. Whilst teaching this activity I asked a few children to do the same activity but using only pencils (2B, HB and 2H) rather than the computer. Once the children had made their animal or character we discussed in the plenary what they had enjoyed most. I then asked two children to show their work (one generated by the computer and the other using pencil) and asked the class which they preferred and why. Is machine generated art as good as hand made art? Which do they prefer making?

National Curriculum Links for Key Stage 2

This activity covers:

Art
1a and 2b
ICT
2a

TOPIC LINKS
∞∞∞∞∞

Dürer
Animal Art
Texture, Tone and Line
Imaginary/Mythological creatures
Collage
Creative Writing

Whole Lotta Warhol

You will need: Microsoft Word and access to information on, and examples of, the work of Andy Warhol.

Here is an opportunity to check out one of the most revolutionary artists of the 20th century. It gives you the chance to explore pattern, shape and colour.

The Task

Check out Andy Warhol on the internet, CD-ROM or at your local library. As you will see, he was really into repeating patterns.

Marilyn (1962) by Andy Warhol

These Warhol-style images can easily be created by simply using 'Clip Art', 'AutoShapes' and 'Background Fill Effects.' Here's how it's done...

Select the rectangle from the 'AutoShapes' menu.

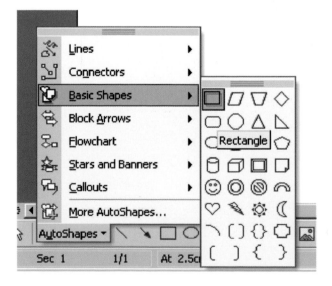

Once you have a square on the page, right-click on it and make a copy. Then paste this second square onto the page as well.

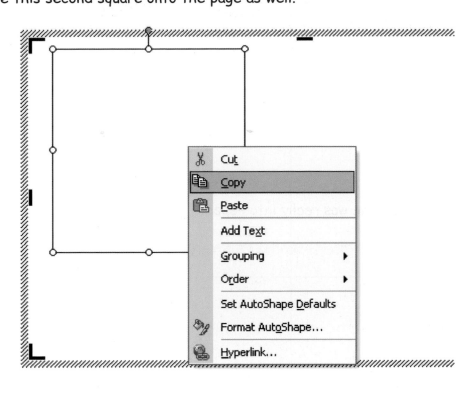

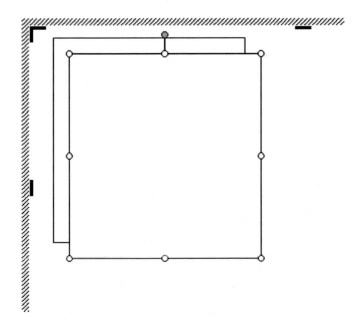

Once you have done this, move the square alongside the first square and continue this process until you have a three by three grid of squares.

Choose other shapes from 'AutoShapes' and place them inside the first square. Copy and paste your shapes into each square

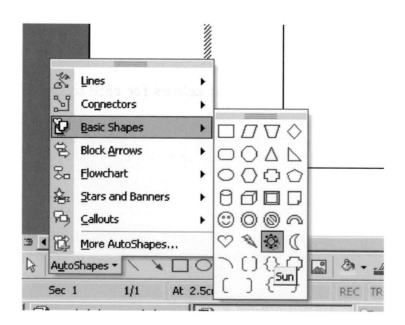

Fill the shapes and the background of the squares with colours from 'Fill Colour'.

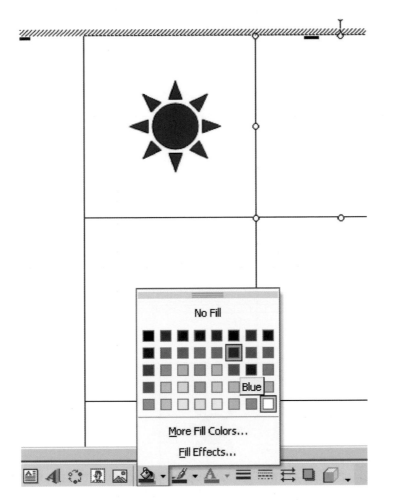

Here I have chosen blue for my sun.

Now experiment with the colours and make shades that appeal to you. They can be complementary, but sometimes contrasting colours can be exciting.

Try using different combinations of colours for each square.

Now you are almost there. Click on a square to experiment with different background effects by going to 'Format', then 'Background', and then 'Fill Effects.' Select 'Two colours', then choose your background colour and shading style.

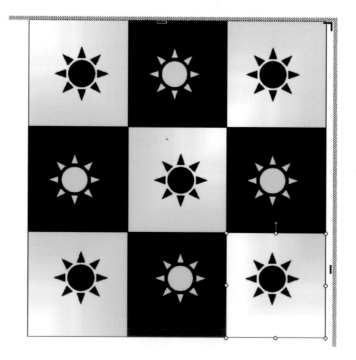

✍ Notes for Parents and Teachers

This activity allows children to discover one of the most revolutionary artists of the 20th century. It allows them to experiment with complementary and contrasting colours and lends itself well to simple colour theory work. The activity also allows pupils to engage with repeating patterns, a KS2 ICT requirement and an integral and ongoing part of the maths curriculum.

This activity can be done as a stand-alone activity or as a group task in the ICT suite. It allows children to explore and become familiar with 'Pop Art' as a genre and be creative within its traditions. It allows for quite sophisticated manipulation of a number of Word facilities and requires children to think about colour combinations and the use of shape and space. It has a relevance to maths as children are required to estimate the amount of space occupied by the overall design. Calculations of area can be done here. Equally, it tackles the concepts of repeating patterns which occur in the KS2 ICT curriculum and are an ongoing strand in the maths curriculum. Andy Warhol once said that everybody would be famous for 15 minutes. A fun extension might be for children to imagine what they might like to be famous for, or what they might do with their 15 minutes of fame. Would they preach for world peace, for example, or have a high octane party? This could provide a great literacy dimension to the task.

Andy Warhol was an American artist who lived from 1928 to 1987. During the early 1960s Andy Warhol used newspapers, comic strips and advertisements as his subject matter to produce work that appears bland and dispassionate. He wanted to encourage the idea that anybody and everybody could produce art, just as if they were a machine. Notable pieces of work were 'do it yourself' canvases with numbers placed in various places, mimicking painting by numbers pictures. For more information look at the Andy Warhol Foundation at *www.warholfoundation.org*

National Curriculum Links

This activity covers:

ICT
1a, 1b, 2a and 5b
Art
4 and 5c

TOPIC LINKS

Warhol
Modern Art
Fame
Shape, Pattern and Colour
Printmaking
Repeating Patterns

Chillin' Uccello

You will need: Microsoft Paint (Click on Start, then follow the link to Programs, then to Accessories, and finally to Paint).

'Niccolo da Tolentino leads the Florentine Troops' 1450s, by Paolo Uccello

The Task

Look at this painting by Uccello. He was famous for the use of perspective in his paintings. Notice how Uccello uses the broken swords and lances on the battleground to create the sense that the picture has real 3-D space. The soldiers also appear smaller, the further away they are. This is called perspective.

You can make your own battle background and make it look real!

Amelia, Year 6

This activity uses the 'Cut and Paste' facility in Paint to generate a mass of trees with the illusion of a forest disappearing into the distance. That is, you can create the impression of perspective in your drawing.

Open the Paint program and make a simple drawing of a plant or tree.

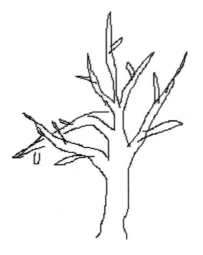

Use the select box to make a dotted line around your drawing. This tells the computer that you only want to work on this part of your drawing.

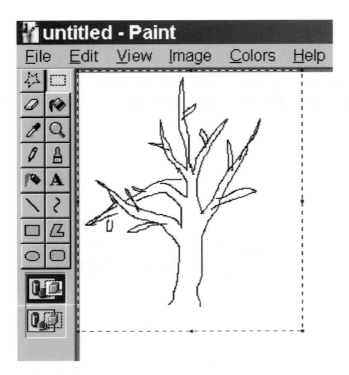

You can now use 'Copy and Paste' to reproduce your drawing. Now click on the 'Background' icon.

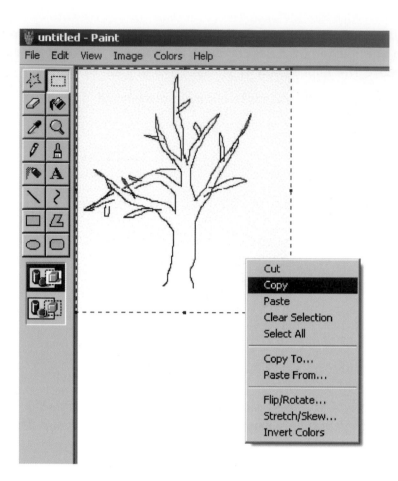

This is the transparent background. It will allow your copied picture not to obscure the picture underneath.

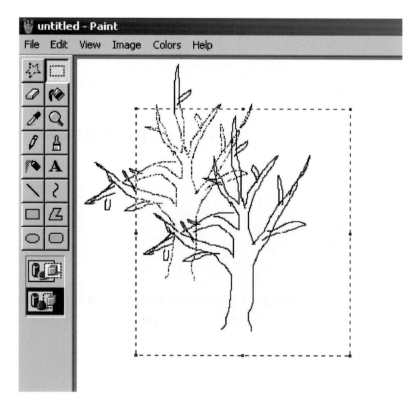

Do this several times until you have lots of trees in your picture. You will need to resize them like I have done in my picture, so that they look like they are disappearing into the distance. You need to do this just after you have pasted the picture on to the page. While it still has the dotted frame, click on one of the corners and drag it to make the frame larger or smaller. Your picture will change size too.

I've added a simple horizon line, which makes the trees look like they are disappearing into the distance.

You could try different types of trees or even plants. Adding colour can really bring your picture alive.

To do this you will need to click on the Brush icon then select a colour from the palette below.

If you make a mistake, you can undo some of your work.

I found it best to use a large brush to colour the larger areas but then changed to a smaller brush when colouring round the branches.

You can print out your battle background and draw your own soldiers onto it, including all the blood and gore!

Challenge

Can you make the tones of the colours stronger the closer the tree appears to you, and weaker the further away they appear? This will really help in creating the illusion of perspective.

✍ Notes for Parents and Teachers

This activity helps children to use the cut and paste facility, which is common to many programs, in an art context. Resizing a drawing is an excellent way to learn how we perceive the world. The first artist to use perspective in his work was Uccello.

If you have access to a projector or interactive whiteboard then demonstrating the resizing of a familiar image to the children would make for a powerful demonstration on perspective. Alternatively, this activity will work with a small group of children using a laptop or classroom computer while the rest of the class use the more traditional pencil and paper.

Uccello was an Italian artist who lived from 1397–1475. You can find out about him on *www.artchive.com*. He is famous for his careful and sophisticated perspective studies. The painting at the beginning of this unit is one of three panels. It commemorates the Battle of San Romano in which the Florentines, under the leadership of Niccolo da Tolentino, defeated the Sienese led by Bernardino della Ciarda. They were intended as decoration for the large hall on the ground floor of the Medici Palace, called Lorenzo's room. The swords and lances left on the battlefield give the picture a sense of depth (perspective).

National Curriculum Links for Key Stage 2

This activity covers:

Art
4a, 4c and 5a
ICT
2a

TOPIC LINKS

Uccello
Perspective
Landscape
Medici – Italian Art

Stunning Stained Glass

You will need: Microsoft Paint and access to information about, and examples of, stained glass windows; information about William Morris; OHP paper (most computer shops and stationers stock this).

Design by Morris and Philip Webb at Church of All Saints, Selsley, Gloucestershire (courtesy Cotswolds Hyperguide Home Page).

The Task

Look up stained glass windows on the internet, CD-ROM or at your local library. Study how the picture is made up of individual blocks. You can make your very own unique stained glass window, using 'Paint' to design your stained glass template. Here's how...

First, click on the Rectangle icon then draw a simple outline for the frame of your design.

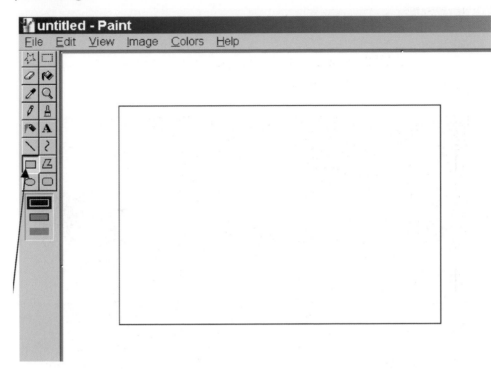

Now continue your design by using the different shape icons. Here I have chosen a circle. You can use the pencil icon to draw freehand if you feel confident enough.

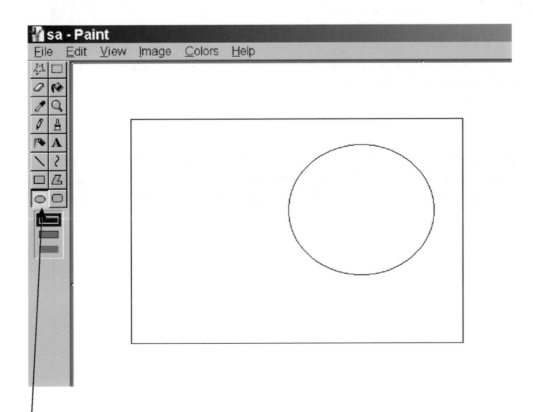

I have added some lines by using the Line icon. Now my sun has its rays!

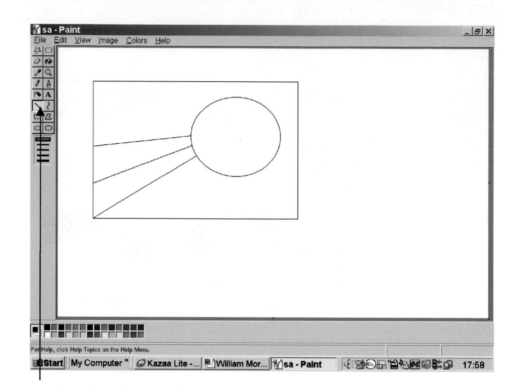

Once you are happy with your design, you can use the Fill with Colour icon to colour your work.

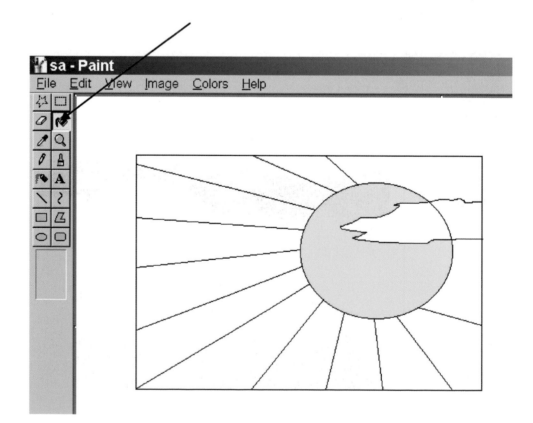

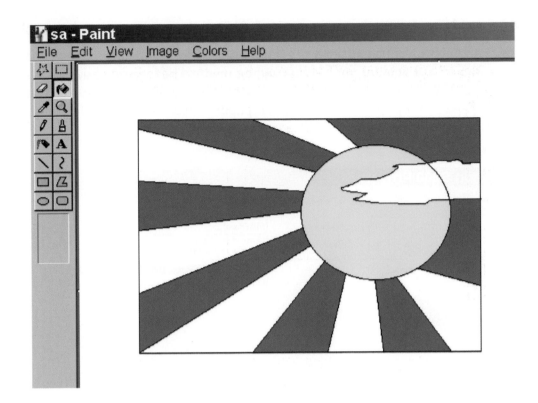

Use the shapes to create a design that you like. Keep it simple to begin with – geometrical designs are often the best to start with.

I needed to erase part of the circle of the sun for the cloud to look right. You can make corrections by using the erase icon. You can also choose the size of your rubber.

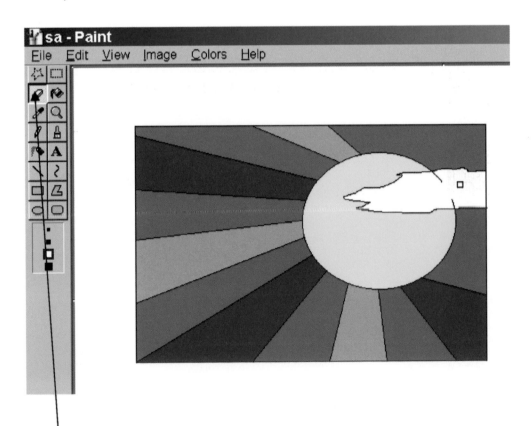

When you have finished, load a piece of OHP paper into your printer.

Select to print your image from the 'File' menu (if you click on the print icon at the top of the toolbar your image will be printed before you have chosen your paper). Then go to the 'Properties' menu. On the Main Page you will see 'Media Type'. It will probably say 'plain paper'. Click on that little window and select 'transparency' or 'OHP' paper from the options available.

Press 'Print' and – bingo! – you have your very own stained glass window.

Cover it with stickyback plastic to protect it from condensation.

✍ Notes for Parents and Teachers

This is a very 'hands-on' and practical art activity that is delivered through the use of ICT. The finished results can be beautiful.

William Morris was an English artist who lived from 1834 to 1896. In 1861 he became involved in the setting up of a firm, Morris, Marshall, Faulkner and Co. This later became simply Morris and Co. The company produced a wide range of decorative arts, including furniture, stained glass and tiles. The best known work is Morris's wallpaper designs of plants, flowers and birds. The William Morris Society *www.morrissociety.org* is a good source of further information. If you go to the bottom of the website and take the link for design you can explore Morris's work.

This task can be done as a stand-alone or as a group activity. It provides the opportunity for children to become familiar with one of the most prominent and widely accomplished artists in English culture. The task can be applied to a number of areas of study: it provides an opportunity for children to become familiar with an ancient tradition of artisanship; it can support studies of the local area, as most local communities will have examples of stained glass windows in their local church; and it provides for study more generally of 'Signs and Symbols' which are part of the National Curriculum requirements in RE. Some schools have even gone so far as to design their own stained glass windows and get them made and installed in their school. This might even involve a visit to a stained glass window workshop. It's great when some of the children's computer generated designs are transformed in this way.

National Curriculum Links to Key Stage 2

Art
2a, 2b and 2c

TOPIC LINKS

William Morris
Glass
Churches
Symbols in Religion
Light
Transparency, Translucency and Opacity
Local Environment

National Curriculum Links

English

Reading

1. To read with fluency, accuracy and understanding, pupils should be taught to use:
   - phonemic awareness and phonic knowledge
   - word recognition and graphic knowledge
   - knowledge of grammatical structures
   - contextual understanding.

Understanding texts

2. Pupils should be taught to:
   - use inference and deduction
   - look for meaning beyond the literal
   - make connections between different parts of a text (for example, how stories begin and end, what has been included and omitted in information writing)
   - use their knowledge of other texts they have read.

Literature

4. To develop understanding and appreciation of literary texts, pupils should be taught to:
   - recognise the choice, use and effect of figurative language, vocabulary and patterns of language
   - identify different ways of constructing sentences and their effects
   - identify how character and setting are created, and how plot, narrative structure and themes are developed.

Non-fiction and non-literary texts

5. To develop understanding and appreciation of non-fiction and non-literary texts, pupils should be taught to:
   - identify the use and effect of specialist vocabulary.

Breadth of study

7. During the key stage, pupils should be taught knowledge, skills and understanding of literature, non-fiction and non-literary texts.

Non-fiction and non-literary texts

9. The range should include:
   - print and ICT-based reference and information materials (for example, textbooks, reports, encyclopaedias, handbooks, dictionaries, thesauruses, glossaries, CD-ROMs, internet).

Knowledge, skills and understanding

Composition

1. Pupils should be taught to:
   - choose form and content to suit a particular purpose (for example, notes to read or organise thinking, plans for action, poetry for pleasure).

Planning and drafting

2. To develop their writing on paper and on screen, pupils should be taught to:
   - proofread – check the draft for spelling and punctuation errors, omissions and repetitions.

Spelling

4. Pupils should be taught:
   - Morphology – the use of appropriate terminology, including vowel, consonant, homophone and syllable.

Breadth of study

9. The range of purposes for writing should include:
   - to imagine and explore feelings and ideas, focusing on creative uses of language and how to interest the reader.

Maths

Knowledge, skills and understanding

Using and applying number
1. Pupils should be taught to:

Problem solving
(c) select and use appropriate mathematical equipment, including ICT
(k) search for pattern in their results; develop logical thinking and explain their reasoning.

Space and shape
(e) read and plot coordinates in the first quadrant, then in all four quadrants (for example, plot the vertices of a rectangle, or a graph of the multiples of 3).

ICT

Knowledge, skills and understanding

Finding things out
1. Pupils should be taught:
   to talk about what information they need and how they can find and use it (for example, searching the internet or a CD-ROM, using printed material, asking people), how to prepare information for development using ICT, including selecting suitable sources, finding information, classifying it and checking it for accuracy (for example, finding information from books or newspapers, creating a class database, classifying by characteristics and purposes, checking the spelling of names is consistent) to interpret information, to check it is relevant and reasonable and to think about what might happen if there were any errors or omissions.

Developing ideas and making things happen

2. Pupils should be taught:
   how to develop and refine ideas by bringing together, organising and reorganising text, tables, images and sound as appropriate (for example, desktop publishing, multimedia presentations).

Exchanging and sharing information

3. Pupils should be taught:

   to be sensitive to the needs of the audience and think carefully about the content and quality when communicating information (for example, work for presentation to other pupils, writing for parents, publishing on the internet).

Reviewing, modifying and evaluating work as it progresses

4. Pupils should be taught to:
   - review what they and others have done to help them develop their ideas
   - describe and talk about the effectiveness of their work with ICT, comparing it with other methods and considering the effect it has on others (for example, the impact made by a desktop-published newsletter or poster)
   - talk about how they could improve future work.

Breadth of study

5. During the key stage, pupils should be taught the knowledge, skills and understanding through:
   - working with a range of information to consider its characteristics and purposes (for example, collecting factual data from the internet and a class survey to compare the findings)
   - working with others to explore a variety of information sources and ICT tools (for example, searching the internet for information about a different part of the world, designing textile patterns using graphics software, using ICT tools to capture and change sounds)
   - investigating and comparing the uses of ICT inside and outside school.

Art

Knowledge, skills and understanding

Exploring and developing ideas

1. Pupils should be taught to:
   - record from experience and imagination, to select and record from first-hand observation and to explore ideas for different purposes
   - question and make thoughtful observations about starting points and select ideas to use in their work.

Investigating and making art, craft and design

2. Pupils should be taught to:
   - investigate and combine visual and tactile qualities of materials and processes and to match these qualities to the purpose of the work
   - apply their experience of materials and processes, including drawing, developing their control of tools and techniques
   - use a variety of methods and approaches to communicate observations, ideas and feelings, and to design and make images and artefacts.

Evaluating and developing work

3. Pupils should be taught to:
   - compare ideas, methods and approaches in their own and others' work and say what they think and feel about them
   - adapt their work according to their views and describe how they might develop it further.

Knowledge and understanding

4. Pupils should be taught about:
   - visual and tactile elements, including colour, pattern and texture, line and tone, shape, form and space, and how these elements can be combined and organised for different purposes
   - materials and processes used in art, craft and design and how these can be matched to ideas and intentions
   - the roles and purposes of artists, craftspeople and designers working in different times and cultures (for example, Western Europe and the wider world).

Breadth of study

5. During the key stage, pupils should be taught the knowledge, skills and understanding through:
   - exploring a range of starting points for practical work (for example, themselves, their experiences, images, stories, drama, music, natural and made objects and environments)
   - working on their own, and collaborating with others, on projects in two and three dimensions and on different scales
   - using a range of materials and processes, including ICT (for example, painting, collage, print making, digital media, textiles, sculpture)
   - investigating art, craft and design in the locality and in a variety of genres, styles and traditions (for example, in original and reproduction form, during visits to museums, galleries and sites, on the internet).